The Avocado
Lovers' Cookbook

Joyce Carlisle

Celestial Arts
P.O. Box 7327
Berkeley, CA 94707

In association with
Blue Ribbon Publishers

First Printing, November 1985
Manufactured in the United States of America

Cover photo by Robert Howard
Cover design by Ken Scott
Edited by Cynthia Heller
Illustrations and Design by Lark Batteau

Library of Congress Catalog Card Number 85-72111

Carlisle, Joyce
    Avocado Lover's Cookbook

ISBN 0-89087-456-5 (pbk)

1 2 3 4 5 — 88 87 86 85

Acknowledgments

This book was written for my husband Joel and our daughter Marie.

Many people have contributed to this book. To mention all of them would take more space than is available. A few are mentioned here.

Denise Woolsey, Betty Sayles, Lindy Graham,
George Goodall, Marcy Schapel, Terry Stransky,
Liz Myers, Cindy Webster, Dan Poynter,
Mindy Bingham, Margaret Maley, Cindy Ritter,
Cheryl Evanoff, Josephine Van Schaick,
Kathy Sturtevant, Marie Myers, Edward Myers,
Lynn Eggelston, Brent Lathrop, Sally Yoerks,
Nancy Schner, Susan Cole, John Lawrence,
Jim Poynter, Janice Magee, Joseph Lauko,
Alexandra Scott, Carole Hansen, Frank Mori,
Stephen Layton, George Mercure and
Vicki Treen.

I would like to give special thanks to the
California Avocado Commission
Calavo Growers of California, and
Cooperative Extension University of California, Santa Barbara County.

Table of Contents

The Avocado Story

The avocado dates back hundreds of years. Called "ahuacalt" by the Aztecs, its origin is associated with parts of South America, Central America and Mexico. An avocado shaped water jar, dated circa 900 A.D., was discovered in the pre-Incan city of Chanchan. In 1526, the first written account of the avocado occurred when the Spanish historian, Gonzalo Hernandez Oviedo, wrote, "In the center of the fruit is a seed like a peeled chestnut. Between this and the rind is the part which is eaten, which is abundant, and is similar to butter."

One hundred twenty-five years later, in 1651, a priest named Barnabe Cobo made a distinction between three strains of avocados. He catalogued what we know today as the Mexican, the Guatemalan and the West Indian avocado strains. In 1848, Henry Dalton planted avocado trees a few miles east of Los Angeles. Today there are no longer any traces of these trees. The first known successful planting of California avocado trees occurred in 1871 when R. B. Ord brought three trees from Mexico and planted them in Santa Barbara (an area which remains abundant in the cultivation of avocados). In 1911, an employee of The West Indies Nursery in Altadena, California, Carl Schmidt, was sent to Mexico to find trees that produced quality avocados. He cut buds from many avocado trees and shipped them home. Most of the buds refused to adapt to their new environment. One bud flourished and survived a freeze in 1913. It was given the Spanish name "Fuerte," meaning strong and vigorous. In 1935, Southern California postman, Rudolph Hass, discovered another variety of avocado. It was a chance seedling that produced this Hass avocado, a dark thick pebbly skinned fruit. His children liked the avocado so much that he patented the variety. This avocado bore during the summer months, just opposite the Fuerte winter variety. Both 'Hass' and 'Fuerte' avocados are predominant on the market today.

California is now the largest producer of avocados in the United States, contributing about 80% of the total supply. The Southern and Central Coastal areas of California, as well as the San Joaquin Valley, are abundant in avocado groves. In the past decade avocado acreage has tripled from 26,000 planted acres in 1973 to 82,000 acres in 1983. Industry voices are estimating a harvest of 500 million pounds of avocados in the early 1980s, up from 50 million pounds in the 1950s.

Handling such a large increase in avocado production has proven to be quite a chore for the California avocado growers. Presently the growers and handlers are exporting their fruit to Japan, Hong Kong, Switzerland, France and England and to the eastern United States. They are hoping increased exports will help handle some of the abundance. A ripening process, recently implemented by the shippers and retailers has been shown to increase sales. This process will provide consumers with ripe avocados in the supermarkets. Growers in the San Joaquin Valley continue to search for new avocado varieties that are more durable, weather and pest resistant and bear more fruit. There are hundreds of varieties under experiment. Florida, Hawaii and Texas also provide the United States with avocados. Other avocado producing countries include Mexico, Brazil, Israel, South Africa, Australia and New Zealand.

Buying, Storing and Ripening Avocados

Avocados are sold in supermarkets across the country. Different varieties mature in different seasons, making avocados available all year.

What to look for when buying avocados

Look for firm, blemishless avocados with the stem button still attached. Keeping the stem button in place prevents bacteria from entering the open end and causing spoilage. Fruit purchased firm has a better chance of ripening evenly and consistently, given gentle care. Some blemishes are caused by sunburn and limb rub and may not affect the interior of the fruit, other blemishes may develop dark bitter areas.

Storing and freezing avocados

Avocados may be stored at room temperature for 2 to 10 days. Avocados placed in the refrigerator may be kept up to several weeks. The ultimate storage temperature for avocados is 45 to 50 degrees F. Leave the seed in a partial avocado for storing. Sprinkle cut edges with lemon or lime juice. Wrap avocado in plastic and refrigerate. Avocado pulp may be frozen. Mash or purée pulp with 1 tablespoon lemon or lime juice per quart pulp. Place in an airtight container and freeze. Frozen avocado pulp will keep for several weeks.

How to ripen avocados

Press the avocado to test for ripeness. It should yield to gentle pressure of the finger tips. Slice out a thin wedge, there should be no resistance to the knife until contacting the seed. Remove the wedge and taste. It should be soft and buttery smooth, if not; squeeze lemon juice over the cut edges, wait another day or two and try again. Speed up the ripening process by placing an avocado, with an orange or apple, in a small paper bag and closing it tightly. Place the bag in a warm, dark area. The concentration of the natural ethylene gasses will cause the avocado to ripen faster. Slow the ripening process by placing an avocado in the refrigerator. To resume ripening, return the fruit to room temperature.

Removing the Seed

Slice the avocado lengthwise around the seed. Place each half in the palms of your hands, gently twist and separate.

Sprinkle the cut edges with lemon juice to prevent the fruit from darkening.

Strike a sharp knife directly into the seed, twist and the seed will lift out.

Slicing, Dicing and Peeling an Avocado

Scoop out balls with a melon baller or carefully dice the avocado in its shell. Use a spoon around the edges to scoop the fruit out. Remember to sprinkle all cut edges with lemon or lime juice to prevent the fruit from darkening.

Peel or pare the skin back. Sometimes the skin will just fall away, if not, cut slits in the skin and peel it like a banana. A spoon may be used around the edges to scoop the fruit out whole. Slice a thin layer from the bottom of the avocado half to prevent it from rolling.

Lay the peeled avocado half with the cut side down and slice to form half rings.

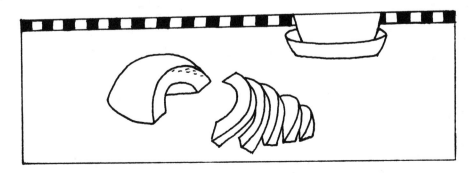

Avocados and Nutrition

The avocado has many vitamins and minerals. It is rich in vitamins A, C, and B6. This richness is unusual even among meats, vegetables, dairy products and grains. Most fruits contain energy in the form of sugars, but not the avocado. It is avocado oil that is packed with energy. Avocados are easy to digest and behind the smooth buttery texture is plenty of fiber. Avocados contain no cholesterol and very little sodium. The nutritional qualities of avocados make them good food for everyone.

Vitamin and Mineral Chart

Per ½ average Avocado (about 3 oz)	% U.S. RDA
Protein	2.0
Vitamin A	10.0
Vitamin C	10.0
B1 Thiamin	6.0
B2 Riboflavin	6.0
B3 Niacin	8.0
B6 Pyridoxine	10.0
Calcium	*
Iron	6.0
Vitamin E	4.0
Folic Acid	15.0
Phosphorus	4.0
Magnesium	8.0
Zinc	2.0
Copper	10.0
Pantothenic Acid	8.0
Calories	150.0
Carbohydrates	2.0gm
Fat	14.0gm
Saturated Fatty Acids	2.0gm
Polyunsaturated Fatty Acids	2.0gm
Cholesterol	0
Sodium	10.0mg
Potassium	540.0mg

Nutrient values are listed from the 1981 edition of USDA Handbook 456 Nutritive Value of American Foods in Common Units.

*Contains less than 2% U.S. RDA

Avocado
Hors d'oeuvres

Raspberry Vinaigrette

Preparation time: 10 minutes, plus 1 hour chill time
Yield: 4 servings

⅓ cup raspberry vinegar*
2 tablespoons sugar
1 cup ripe raspberries
⅔ cup salad oil
1 inch cinnamon stick
2 avocados, sliced

Mix vinegar and sugar. Pour mixture into a shaker, add raspberries, cinnamon stick and oil. Shake vigorously. Place avocados on a serving dish. Pour vinaigrette over avocado slices, coating the avocado. Chill for 1 hour.

*Available in specialty food stores.

Melon Balls

with Ginger Dip

Preparation time: 10 minutes
Yield: 4 servings

1 *cantaloupe melon, scooped into balls*
½ *honeydew melon, scooped into balls*
2 *avocados, scooped into balls*
  lemon juice
  lettuce leaves

Gently toss melon balls and avocados together. Place on lettuce leaves. Sprinkle generously with lemon juice. Chill.

Ginger Dip

8 *oz. cream cheese, softened*
¼ *cup milk*
2 *tablespoons honey*
3 *tablespoons lemon juice*
1 *teaspoon fresh grated ginger*
  (½ teaspoon dried, ground)

Combine cream cheese, milk, honey, lemon juice and ginger. Stir until smooth. Spoon dressing over salad and serve.

Strawberry, Pineapple and Cheese Kabobs

Preparation time: 15 minutes
Yield: 8 kabobs

  2 avocados, sliced into eight wedges
     then halved to make 16 pieces each
16 melon balls (cantaloupe, honeydew, crenshaw)
16 cheddar cheese cubes (1 inch)
16 fresh strawberries, washed and stemmed
16 pineapple chunks (1 inch)
  8 wood skewers
  4 limes, quartered

Assemble fruit and cheese onto skewers using 2 pieces of each. Generously squeeze limes over kabobs. Serve.

Dilled Cucumber

Preparation time: 10 minutes
Yield: 4 servings

Dill

1 medium cucumber, thinly sliced
  (peeled if skin is tough or waxed)
1 medium red onion, thinly sliced
2 avocados, sliced
¼ cup cider vinegar
½ cup salad oil
2 teaspoons fresh dill weed
  (½ teaspoon dried, crumbled)
1 clove garlic, minced
  freshly ground black pepper to taste
  lettuce leaves

Place cucumbers, onions and avocados in a shallow dish. Combine vinegar, oil and seasonings. Whip with a wire whisk until mixed. Pour mixture over cucumbers, onions and avocados. Chill 2 hours. Turn occasionally. Serve on lettuce leaves.

Dill is an annual herb. It has feathery leaves with a pungent seed. Dill leaves may be used in salads, stews, sauces and on fish. The seeds are used in pickles and vinegars. Dill will keep well dried or frozen, be sure to leave the stems on for freezer storage.

Stuffed Celery Sticks with Peanuts

Preparation time: 10 minutes
Yield: 16 sticks

1 avocado, mashed
¼ cup grated carrots
¼ cup raisins
1 teaspoon lemon juice
8 celery ribs, halved crosswise
¼ cup chopped peanuts

Mix avocado, carrots, raisins and lemon juice. Spoon into celery stick centers. Sprinkle with peanuts and serve.

Ham and Swiss Spears

Preparation time: 10 minutes
Yield: 20 spears

2 avocados, cut into ¾ inch pieces
½ lb. cooked ham cut into ½ inch cubes
½ lb. Swiss cheese cut into ½ inch cubes
20 pitted black olives
20 wooden skewers
lime wedges
crackers

Spear an avocado cube, an olive, a ham cube and a cheese cube with skewer. Sprinkle with lime juice. Serve with crackers.

Avocado Fondue

Preparation time: 20 minutes
Yield: 4 to 6 servings

4 *tablespoons butter*
1 *medium onion, chopped fine*
½ *cup flour*
1 *cup milk*
½ *cup half and half*
   salt to taste
   freshly ground black pepper
4 *tablespoons lemon juice*
1 *avocado, mashed*
½ *cup parmesan cheese*
1 *tablespoon brandy*
   lightly steamed vegetable sticks
   shrimp, cooked and cleaned
   French bread cut into cubes

Melt butter in a saucepan over medium heat. Sauté onion until translucent. Lower heat, stir in flour and cook for 2 minutes. Add milk, half and half, seasonings, lemon juice, and cheese. Stir until heated through, do not boil. Stir in brandy and avocado. Pour into fondue server. Serve with vegetable sticks, shrimp and bread cubes for dipping.

Quesadillas

with Tomato Salsa
(pronounced: key-sah-thee-yas)

Preparation time: 15 minutes
Yield: 4 servings

4 flour tortillas
4 tablespoons butter
1½ cups shredded cheese
   (jack or cheddar)

Melt butter in a wide round skillet over medium high heat. Place one tortilla in skillet, sprinkle cheese onto one half of tortilla. Fold tortilla over and press flat, move to one side of pan. Place another tortilla in the pan (it won't lie flat) and repeat the process. Brown both sides. Place quesadillas in warm oven until served.

Tomato Salsa

2 medium tomatoes, chopped
2 scallions, sliced
1 (4 oz.) can diced green chiles
¼ cup fresh cilantro leaves
   (2 tablespoons dried, crumbled)
1 avocado, sliced
½ cup sour cream

Toss tomatoes, scallions, chiles and cilantro together. Place avocado slices on hot quesadillas. Drop on sour cream. Spoon salsa over and serve.

Avocado Tempura

with Sweet and Sour Apricot Sauce

Preparation time: 20 minutes
Yield: 4 servings

2 avocados, sliced

Batter:

1 egg, separated
6 tablespoons flat beer
⅓ cup flour
½ teaspoon dried, ground mustard seed
(1 ½ teaspoons prepared mustard)
⅛ teaspoon black pepper

Combine beaten egg yolk with beer, flour, mustard and pepper. Stir until well blended. Just before cooking, beat egg white until stiff (not dry). Fold into batter.

Heat 1 inch cooking oil in large skillet on medium high heat until fragrant. Dip avocado slices into batter and fry, turning to brown evenly (2 or 3 minutes each side). Remove from skillet and drain briefly on paper towels. Serve.

Sweet and Sour Apricot Sauce

½ cup apricot preserves
2 tablespoons cider vinegar

Mix well. Chill until served.

The mustard plant is a summer annual. Its leaves are used as green vegetables and the seeds are ground into spices. Dry mustard is the residue of the seed after the oil has been expressed. Mustard seed may be used whole in pickling or ground in omelettes, relishes and salad dressings.

Hot Stuffed Chiles

California chiles range from sweet to mildly hot. Canned chiles are easy to find in the supermarket. They are labeled "Whole Chiles." When fresh chiles are used they should be firm and shiny. They must be toasted and the skins removed. Preheat broiler. Wash, dry and place chiles on broiler rack 1 inch from heat source. Watch closely and turn until chiles are blistered and browned evenly. Removed from heat and place them in a plastic bag. Cool for about 10 minutes. Catch the skin at the loose points with a sharp knife and peel them one at a time, leaving the remaining chiles in the plastic bag. Be careful not to tear the chiles. Cut the stems off for stuffing.

Preparation time: 15 minutes using canned chiles
30 minutes using fresh chiles
Yield: 12 stuffed chiles

12 **whole chiles**
 8 **oz. cream cheese, softened**
 2 **avocados, mashed**
 2 **cloves garlic, minced**
    (½ teaspoon garlic powder)
¼ **cup minced onion**
 1 **tablespoon lemon juice**
 1 **bunch cilantro sprigs**
¼ **cup chopped black olives**
 2 **lbs. tortilla chips**

Cut chiles in half lengthwise and remove seeds. Blend cream cheese with avocado, garlic, onion and lemon juice. With a piping bag, pipe mixture into each chile half. Serve on a platter lined with cilantro sprigs. Garnish with chopped olives. Serve at room temperature with tortilla chips.

Make a quick piping bag by using a strong plastic bag. Fill the corner with filling and cut the tip off.

Chicken and Grape Canapés

Preparation time: 10 minutes
Yield: 16 canapés

1½ *cups cooked chicken*
½ *cup seedless grapes, halved lengthwise*
1 *avocado, diced*
3 *tablespoons slivered almonds*
¼ *cup mayonnaise (yogurt or sour cream)*
2 *teaspoons lemon juice*
⅛ *teaspoon cayenne pepper*
dash white pepper

Toss together chicken, grapes, avocado and almonds. Mix mayonnaise, lemon juice and peppers. Pour mixture over chicken and toss again. Serve on toast.

Shrimp and Avocado Mousse with Caviar

Caviar is the roe of fish. It is a variety of colors. Red and pink caviar are roe of salmon, cod, carp, pike or tuna. Other caviars are roe of sturgeon. All caviar should be translucent, firm and perfectly whole. Never serve caviar in a metal dish, it will acquire a metallic taste.

Preparation time: 25 minutes, plus 2 ½ hours chill time
Yield: 6 to 8 servings

1 *envelope unflavored gelatin*
1 *cup cold water*
1 *tablespoon orange juice*
⅛ *teaspoon cayenne pepper*
2 *large avocados, mashed*
⅔ *cup sour cream*
⅓ *cup mayonnaise*
¼ *cup lemon juice*
½ *lb. cooked shrimp, chopped*
2 *teaspoons minced scallion*
   lettuce leaves
   lemon slices
½ *lb. cooked shrimp, whole*
3 *tablespoons chopped scallion*
1 *(2 oz.) jar of caviar*

Place the cold water in a saucepan. Mix in gelatin. Heat slowly and stir until gelatin dissolves. Stir in orange juice and cayenne pepper. Chill until syrupy (about 30 minutes). Stir together avocado, sour cream, mayonnaise and lemon juice. Fold in shrimp and scallion. Pour into a 3½ cup mold that has been oiled and chilled. Chill uncovered until firm (about 2 hours). Unmold onto a lettuce lined platter and garnish with lemon, shrimp, chopped scallion and caviar. Serve with crackers or French bread.

Clean, oil and chill molds before placing any food in them. Unmold by using a thin knife at several points on the edge to release the vaccuum, then turn the mold onto the serving dish. If the food is not released, gently shake it back and forth with hands braced on the serving dish. If the food is still not released, place a warm towel over the bottom of the mold for a few seconds. This will release the molded food although it may cause the gelatin to melt slightly.

Ceviche

Ceviche is a South American favorite. The flavor and texture of fish gently marinated in lime juice is a welcome change from the overcooked seafood we so often encounter. Fresh fish is always best. To keep fresh fish longer than a day or two, wrap it in plastic and pack it in ice. Rinse and pat the fish dry before using.

Preparation time: 20 minutes, plus 24 hours chill time
Yield: 4 servings

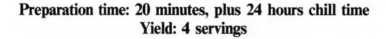

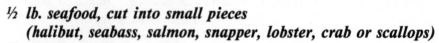

½ lb. seafood, cut into small pieces
  (halibut, seabass, salmon, snapper, lobster, crab or scallops)
½ cup lime juice
1 avocado, diced
2 tablespoons chopped scallion
1 medium tomato, seeded and chopped
3 tablespoons fresh cilantro leaves
  (1 tablespoon dried, crumbled)
2 tablespoons diced green chiles
1 tablespoon salad oil
1 tablespoon red wine
1 tablespoon fresh oregano, chopped
  (1 teaspoon dried, crumbled)

Cilantro

Marinate fish in lime juice overnight. Gently toss avocado, onions, tomatoes, cilantro and green chiles with fish mixture. Combine oil, wine and oregano. Pour oil mixture over fish and gently toss again. Chill until served.

Cilantro, *also known as Chinese parsley, is an herb grown from coriander seeds. It has thin short stems and round, lightly fringed leaves. The flavor and smell of cilantro are quite pungent. Fresh cilantro is delicious in salads, chicken dishes, salsas, Mexican and Chinese dishes. Cilantro shouldn't be chopped, instead remove the stems and use the leaves whole or torn.*

Fishy smells: *Eliminate fishy smells by keeping a dishpan of water and vinegar (1 gallon water, ¼ cup vinegar) at hand to rinse knives and cutting boards while working with fish.*

Clam Cocktail

Chopped clams are available at the supermarket in the canned fish section or the gourmet food section. If fresh clams are used, they must be cleaned and opened. Place fresh clams in salt water for 15 to 20 minutes to release sand and mud. Scrub them with a stiff brush. Change the water and repeat the process 2 or 3 times. Freshly dug and store bought clams must be checked and dead ones discarded. Live hard shell clams with gaping shells should close when touched. Soft shell clams are alive if there is some constriction of the siphon or neck when touched. Arrange the scrubbed clams in a wide pan and pour boiling water over them to 1 inch deep. Cover and steam them over medium heat until the shells open (5 to 10 minutes). Remove the clams as they open and set them aside to cool. Remove the meat from the shell with a fork. Larger clams may need extra trimming.

Preparation time: 20 minutes
Yield: 6 servings

2 **avocados, diced**
2 **medium tomatoes, diced**
¼ **cup chopped onion**
¼ **cup chopped celery**
1 **cup chopped cooked clams**
½ **cup clam juice or fish stock***
⅛ **cup ketchup**
3 **tablespoons lemon juice**
  dash of Tobasco sauce
1 **teaspoon Worcestershire sauce**
¼ **teaspoon horseradish sauce**

Toss avocados, tomatoes, onions, celery, clams and clam juice. Combine remaining ingredients and toss with clam mixture. Chill. Serve in cocktail glasses.

*Please read about stocks on page 73.

Crispy Bacon Wraps

Preparation time: 15 minutes
Yield: 18 wraps

1 avocado, cut into ¾ inch cubes
   lemon juice, sprinkled over avocado
9 slices of bacon (about ½ lb.), halved
   toothpicks

Cook bacon over low heat until fat is rendered but bacon is not yet crisp. Drain on paper towel. Wrap partially cooked bacon around avocado cubes and secure with toothpicks. Preheat broiler. Place appetizers on broiling rack 2 inches from heat source and broil for 2 minutes. Turn appetizers over and broil for 2 more minutes or until crisp. Drain on paper towel. Serve in a lined basket.

Start cooking bacon in a cold skillet and cook it over low, even heat. The bacon won't curl and most of the splattering is prevented. Cooking bacon slowly also leaves time for other food preparation.

Avocado Dips and Toppings

Guacamole

Preparation time: 10 minutes
Yield: 2 cups

2 avocados, mashed
1 tablespoon lemon juice
1 medium tomato, finely chopped
1 medium onion, finely chopped
¼ cup canned green chiles, finely chopped

Combine avocado and lemon juice. Fold in tomatoes, onions and chiles. Chill. Serve with tortilla chips and fresh vegetable sticks or use as topping for eggs, enchiladas or baked potatoes.

Cream Cheese and Chervil Dip

Chervil is a member of the parsley family. It has a mild celery like flavor. Chopped fresh, it is delicious in green salads, sauces and dips. Substitute chervil in any recipe that calls for parsley.

Preparation time: 10 minutes
Yield: 2 cups and Toppings

1 avocado, mashed
1 tablespoon lime juice
8 oz cream cheese, softened
   dash of cayenne pepper
   salt to taste
2 tablespoons fresh chervil leaves
   (½ teaspoon dried, crumbled)
1 tablespoon finely chopped onion

Chervil

Combine avocado, lemon juice, cream cheese, cayenne and salt. Fold in chervil and onion. Chill. Servce with crackers, vegetable sticks or french bread.

Curry and Coconut Dip

Curry powder is a combination of dried and ground spices and vegetables. There are as many combinations of curry powder as there are vegetables. Curry powder can be used in many dishes including lamb, fish, beef, seafood, poultry, beans and rice.

Preparation time: 10 minutes
Yield: 1½ cups

1 avocado, mashed
1 tablespoon lemon juice
2 tablespoons mayonnaise
½ teaspoon curry powder
salt to taste
¼ cup grated coconut

Combine avocado, lemon juice, mayonnaise, curry and salt. Fold in coconut. Chill. Serve with fresh fruit and crackers or use as a topping for chicken and fish dishes.

Lemon Caper Dip

A caper is a tiny unopened flower bud of a small prickly Mediterranean shrub. Capers are pickled in vinegar and stored in small bottles. They are usually found in the condiment section at the supermarket. Capers will keep for months in the refrigerator.

Preparation time: 10 minutes
Yield: 2 cups

2 avocados, mashed
2 tablespoons lemon juice
2 tablespoons capers
2 tablespoons finely chopped onion

Combine avocado and lemon juice. Fold in capers and onion. Chill. Serve with crackers, vegetable sticks or as a topping for seafood dishes.

Creamy Cucumber Dip

Preparation time: 10 minutes
Yield: 2 cups

2 avocados, mashed
2 tablespoons lemon juice
2 teaspoons fresh dill weed
   (½ teaspoon dried, crumbled)
1 clove garlic, crushed
   (¼ teaspoon powder)
¼ cup chopped scallions
½ cup chopped and peeled cucumber

Combine avocado, lemon juice, dill and garlic. Fold in scallions and cucumbers. Chill. Serve with chips and vegetable sticks or use as a topping for sliced tomatoes.

Seafood Dip

Preparation time: 10 minutes
Yield: 2 cups
1 avocado, mashed
2 tablespoons lemon juice
½ cup sour cream or yogurt
   salt to taste
1 cup cooked and chopped seafood
   (halibut, seabass, salmon, snapper, lobster, crab, shrimp or
   scallops)

Combine avocado, lemon juice, sour cream and salt. Fold in seafood. Chill. Serve with chips, vegetable sticks, crackers or as a spread on sandwiches.

Garlic Bacon Dip

Preparation time: 20 minutes
Yield: 2 cups

2 *avocados, mashed*
3 *tablespoons lemon juice*
⅛ *teaspoon cayenne pepper*
2 *cloves garlic, crushed*
   (½ teaspoon powder)
½ *lb. bacon, cooked and crumbled*

Combine avocado, lemon juice, cayenne pepper and garlic. Fold in bacon. Chill. Serve with chips, vegetable sticks or as a topping for eggs and baked pototoes.

Roquefort Bacon Dip

Preparation time: 10 minutes
Yield: 3 cups

2 *avocados, mashed*
1 *tablespoon lemon juice*
½ *cup sour cream or yogurt*
2 *tablespoons chopped chives*
   (scallion tops may be substituted)
3 *slices bacon, cooked and crumbled*
⅓ *cup Roquefort cheese, crumbled*

Combine avocado, lemon juice and sour cream. Fold in chives, bacon and cheese. Chill. Serve with chips, vegetable sticks or bread.

Garlic cloves are easily peeled by pressing the side of a wide flat knife to a clove. Applying pressure and gently rolling the clove will crack the skin and cause it to easily fall away.

A ceramic garlic keeper absorbs moisture and keeps a cool environment. A terra cotta flower pot with saucer may be substituted. Place the garlic in the saucer and invert the pot over the saucer.

Avocado Butters

Lime and Ginger Butter Ball

with Hazelnuts

Hazelnuts, also called filbert nuts, are perishable when fresh. Store them in the freezer. If nuts are tough, spread them on a baking sheet and toast them for 10 to 15 minutes at 350 degrees. The skins will dry and easily flake off.

Preparation time: 10 minutes
Yield: 1½ cups

1 avocado, mashed
2 tablespoons lemon juice
2 teaspoons grated fresh ginger
(1 teaspoon dried, ground or 2 tablespoons ginger syrup)
½ lb. sweet butter, softened
1 cup chopped hazelnuts

Blend avocado, lemon juice and ginger. Add butter until blended. Form into ball and chill. Spread hazelnuts on wax paper. Roll butter ball until evenly coated. Serve with crackers.

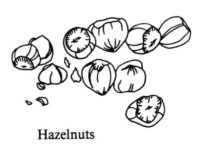

Hazelnuts

Herb Butter

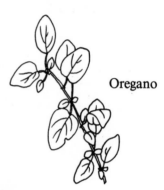

Oregano

Preparation time: 5 minutes, 1 hour chill time
Yield: 1½ cups

1 avocado, mashed
2 tablespoons lemon juice
1 teaspoon each fresh parsley, oregano, savory and tarragon leaves, finely chopped
(½ teaspoon each dried, crumbled)
½ lb. sweet butter, softened

Mix avocado, lemon juice and herbs. Add butter until well blended. Chill. Serve with any dish in the place of butter.

Oregano is a perennial herb shrub with medium size oval leaves. It has a pungent flavor. Oregano creates a deep rich flavor in meats and tomato sauces, sausages, lamb and pork dishes. It is especially good in Italian and Spanish dishes and is delicious in green salads.

Lemon Butter

Preparation time: 5 minutes, 1 hour chill time
Yield: 1½ cups

1 avocado, mashed
2 tablespoons lemon juice
½ lb. sweet butter, softened

Blend avocado with lemon juice. Add butter until well blended. Shape into rectangular sticks and chill. Serve with toast, vegetables, crackers or seafood.

Make individual butter pats by forming butter into rectangular sticks, chill, then slice with an egg slicer. Make butter balls by scooping chilled butter with a melon baller.

Tarragon Butter

Tarragon *is a perennial herb that grows slowly by creeping rizomes. It has narrow gray-green, aromatic leaves. Tarragon is indispensible in the kitchen. It may be used in eggs, vinegar, freshly made mayonnaise, sauces, cheese and fish dishes.*

Tarragon

Preparation time: 5 minutes, 1 hour chill time
Yield: 1½ cups

1 avocado, mashed
2 tablespoons lemon juice
¼ cup fresh tarragon leaves
 (3 tablespoons dried, crumbled)
½ lb. sweet butter, softened

Mix avocado, lemon juice and tarragon leaves. Add butter until well blended. Shape into rectangular sticks and chill. Serve with vegetables, crackers or seafood.

Fresh Avocado
Salads

Oranges and Almonds

with Sour Cream Dressing

Preparation time: 15 minutes
Yield: 6 servings

  4 *oranges, sectioned*
  2 *avocados, sliced*
  6 *lettuce leaves*

1½ *cups sour cream*
  2 *tablespoons mayonnaise*
  1 *teaspoon grated orange peel*
  ¼ *teaspoon nutmeg*
    salt to taste
  ½ *cup slivered almonds*

Layer avocado and oranges on lettuce lined serving dish. Chill. Combine sour cream, mayonnaise, orange peel, nutmeg and salt. Spoon onto salads. Sprinkle with almonds. Serve.

Cantaloupe and Avocado

with Ginger Honey Dressing

Preparation time: 15 minutes
Yield: 6 servings

2 avocados, scooped into balls
1 medium size cantaloupe melon, scooped into balls
6 large lettuce leaves

Gently toss melon and avocado together. Spoon mixture onto lettuce leaves. Chill.

Ginger

Ginger Honey Dressing

8 oz. cream cheese, softened
¼ cup milk
2 tablespoons honey
3 tablespoons lemon juice
2 teaspoons grated fresh ginger
  (½ teaspoon dried, ground or
  3 tablespoons ginger syrup)

Whip all ingredients together until smooth. Spoon dressing over salad and serve.

Ginger, the root of the perennial plant, Zingiber officinale, must be harvested at the right time or it will be fiberous and bitter. Whole fresh ginger must be kept dry or it will sprout and be useless for flavoring. Ginger may be kept in the refrigerator, in a plastic bag, for about three weeks. Grate, slice or mash the fresh ginger to use in recipes. Dry ginger may be cut into ½ inch pieces and steeped for several hours in cold water. The liquid is used for seasoning. Boiled and preserved in syrup or honey, it is known as Canton Ginger. Chopped fine, this milder form may be used in desserts or sauces with or without the syrup. Use ½ teaspoon ground dried ginger to 1 teaspoon grated fresh ginger or 2 tablespoons ginger syrup.

Melon Salad

with Strawberry Yogurt Dressing

Preparation time: 15 minutes
Yield: 6 servings

3 *avocados, scooped into balls*
6 *cups melon balls (watermelon, cantaloupe or honeydew)*
¼ *cup lime juice*
1 *lb. cottage cheese*
1 *bunch lettuce leaves*

Gently toss avocado and melon together. Sprinkle with lime juice. Spoon fruit onto lettuce leaves. Set scoops of cottage cheese among fruit and chill.

Strawberry Yogurt Dressing

1 *cup sliced strawberries*
1½ *cups yogurt*
¼ *teaspoon grated lemon peel*

Blend all ingredients until smooth. Generously spoon dressing over salad and serve.

Drying and storing lettuce: *Wet lettuce may be dried by placing it in a clean pillowcase and twirling it outdoors. Wrap it in a damp towel and chill. For longer storage, wrap it in towels and plastic, keep it in the vegetable drawer.*

Orange and Watercress Salad

with Sunflower Seed Dressing

Preparation time: 15 minutes
Yield: 4 servings

4 oranges, peeled and sliced round
1 avocado, diced
1 bunch watercress

Place orange and avocado pieces on watercress lined serving dish. Chill.

Sunflower Seed Dressing

Watercress

4 tablespoons salad oil
4 tablespoons orange juice
1 tablespoon cider vinegar
½ teaspoon celery seed
4 teaspoons sunflower seeds

Whisk or shake all ingredients until well blended. Pour evenly over salad and serve. Leftover dressing will be delicious on any salad. Keep refrigerated up to two weeks.

Watercress is a small perennial plant with dime size dark green leaves that grows along running streams. Its flavor is spicy and peppery. It is delicious in fruit salads, green salads, dips and with seafood. Watercress has twice the nutrition of lettuce. Watercress may be stored in the refrigerator with the stems immersed in water. Before using, clip off the tough ends of stems and serve with tender stems attached.

Persimmon Salad

with Pecan and Lime Cream Dressing

Persimmon is a fruit native to China. The acorn shaped Hachuja is the most familiar variety. Buy persimmons that are soft. If soft persimmons are not available, place a hard persimmon in a plastic container with the stem up, pour a drop or two of any liquor (rum, brandy) on the crown. Close the container tight and allow fruit to soften 3 to 6 days.

Preparation time: 15 minutes
Yield: 6 servings

    4 *avocados, sliced*
    2 *large grapefruit, sectioned*
    4 *unpeeled persimmons, quartered*
       lettuce leaves

Arrange avocado, grapefruit and persimmon sections alternately on lettuce leaves. Chill.

Lime Cream Dressing

    2 *cups sour cream or yogurt*
    2 *tablespoons sugar*
    ⅛ *teaspoon grated lime peel*
    6 *tablespoons lime juice*
    ¼ *cup chopped pecans*

Mix sour cream, sugar, lime peel and juice until well blended. Spoon dressing over fruit. Sprinkle with pecans and serve.

Hearts of Palm and Papaya

with Allspice Dressing

Hearts of Palm are taken from the palmetto tree. The heart is cylindrical shaped and fiberous. They are canned and usually found in the gourmet section of supermarkets. They may be sliced or served whole in salads or on relish trays. *Papaya* trees are native to tropical America. They grow where the soil stays warm. Green papaya fruit turns yellow and orange as it ripens. It is eaten like a melon, the seeds may be used as a garnish or seasoning.

Preparation time: 15 minutes
Yield: 6 servings

1 *bunch watercress, trimmed and chilled*
6 *lettuce leaves*
1 *14 oz. can hearts of palm, drained and sliced in ½ inch slices*
1 *papaya, seeded and sliced*
2 *avocados, sliced*

Layer lettuce, then watercress on serving dish. Place papaya and avocado on lettuce. Place hearts of palm among fruit. Chill.

Allspice Dressing

⅓ *cup mayonnaise (yogurt or sour cream)*
2 *tablespoons lime juice*
¼ *teaspoon ground coriander*
¼ *teaspoon ground allspice*

Blend all ingredients until smooth. Spoon over salad and serve. Leftover dressing may be kept up to two weeks.

Grapefruit and Dates

with Nutmeg Dressing

Preparation time: 15 minutes
Yield: 6 servings

3 avocados, quartered
1 grapefruit, sectioned
1 orange, sectioned
1 bunch lettuce

Toss avocados, grapefruit and oranges. Spoon onto lettuce leaves. Chill.

Nutmeg Dressing

1 cup sour cream or yogurt
½ teaspoon grated orange peel
2 tablespoons orange juice
salt to taste
¼ teaspoon ground nutmeg
½ cup chopped, pitted dates
nutmeg

Nutmeg

Blend sour cream, orange peel, juice, salt and nutmeg. Fold in dates. Spoon dressing over salad. Sprinkle with nutmeg and serve.

***Nutmeg and mace** come from the same tough husked fruit, Myristica fragrans. The nut may be used fresh and whole or dried and ground. The lacy outer membrane of the nut is ground into mace. Mace and nutmeg have full rich flavors, use them sparingly.*

Hot Sweet and Sour Salad

Preparation time: 20 minutes
Yield: 6 servings

2 medium avocados, diced
2 medium tomatoes, diced
1 tablespoon fresh cilantro leaves
*   (1 teaspoon dried, crumbled)*
4 slices of bacon
1 medium onion, thinly sliced
4 tablespoons vinegar
1 tablespoon sugar
*   dash of cayenne pepper*

Toss avocados, tomatoes and cilantro gently. Set aside. Cook bacon until crisp. Drain on paper towels. Sauté onion in bacon drippings until tender. Add vinegar, sugar and cayenne pepper. Bring to boil. Pour hot dressing over salad. Sprinkle with crumbled bacon and serve.

Stuffed Tomatoes

Preparation time: 10 minutes
Yield: 4 servings

4 medium tomatoes
1 avocado, mashed
1 tablespoon lemon juice
2 tablespoons minced scallion with tops
1 clove garlic, crushed
1 tablespoon mayonnaise or yogurt
* lettuce leaves*

Cut out the top and centers of tomatoes. Retain pulp. Turn upside down to drain. Combine pulp, avocado, lemon juice, scallions, garlic and mayonnaise, mix well. Fill tomato centers. Place on lettuce leaves and serve.

Chicken and Tomato Salad

with Vinaigrette Dressing

Preparation time: 20 minutes
Yield: 6 servings

1 head lettuce, torn into bite size pieces
1 cup watercress, coarsely chopped
2 tablespoons chopped scallions
2 avocados, sliced
½ cup Roquefort cheese, crumbled
2 cups cooked, diced chicken
1 tomato, diced
6 slices bacon, cooked crisp and crumbled
1 egg, cooked hard and sliced

Toss lettuce, watercress and scallions together in large salad bowl. Arrange avocado slices on lettuce around outer edge of bowl. Sprinkle with cheese. Spoon chicken and tomato into center. Garnish with bacon and egg. Chill.

Vinaigrette Dressing

½ cup wine vinegar
2 tablespoons lemon juice
1 clove garlic, crushed
¾ teaspoon dry mustard
   (2 teaspoons prepared)
1 ½ teaspoons Worcestershire sauce
   salt to taste
   freshly ground black pepper to taste
1 cup salad oil
½ cup olive oil

Combine vinegar, lemon juice and seasonings in a shaker. Shake well. Add oil. Shake until well mixed. Pour dressing over salad and serve.

Turkey and Asparagus Salad

with Creamy Mustard Dressing

Preparation time: 25 minutes
Yield: 6 servings

½ lb. asparagus spears, steamed until tender
½ lb. sliced, cooked turkey, cut into strips
2 avocados, sliced
3 grapefruits, sectioned
1 head lettuce, torn into bite size pieces

Steam asparagus by placing it in a 1 lb. coffee can with 1 inch of water. Set the can into a deep pot with 2 inches of water. Cover and cook over low heat until the desired tenderness is reached. Place asparagus spears, turkey, avocados and grapefruit sections on lettuce. Chill.

Creamy Mustard Dressing

2 tablespoons prepared mustard
salt to taste
1 cup half and half
1 avocado, mashed

Blend all ingredients. Spoon dressing over salad and serve.

Ham Salad

Preparation time: 15 minutes
Yield: 6 servings

1 bunch lettuce leaves
2 avocados, sliced
3 tablespoons lemon juice
½ cup vinegar
2 tablespoons fresh herbs, finely chopped
(2 teaspoons dried, crumbled)
1 ½ lbs. baked ham, torn into bite size pieces
6 medium tomatoes, quartered
1 red onion, thinly sliced
1 bunch watercress, washed and trimmed

Layer lettuce leaves in serving bowl. Arrange avocado slices around outer edge of bowl. Sprinkle with lemon juice. Chill. Combine vinegar and herbs in a mixing bowl. Add ham, tomatoes and onion. Toss gently. Spoon mixture onto lettuce. Garnish with watercress.

Avocado
Salad Dressings

Yogurt and Chervil Salad Dressing

Preparation time: 5 minutes
Yield: 2 cups

1 avocado, mashed
1 tablespoon lemon juice
1 cup yogurt or sour cream
   dash of cayenne pepper
   salt to taste
2 tablespoons fresh chervil, chopped
   (½ teaspoon dried, crumbled)
1 tablespoon finely chopped onion

Stir all ingredients together with a wire whisk. Chill.

Honey and Lime Salad Dressing

Preparation time: 5 minutes
Yield: 2 cups

1 avocado, mashed
2 tablespoons lime juice
1 cup sour cream or yogurt
½ teaspoon grated lime peel
3 tablespoons honey

Blend all ingredients until creamy. Chill. Serve on fruit salads.

Lemon Herb Salad Dressing

Preparation time: 5 minutes
Yield: 2 cups

1 avocado, mashed
¼ cup red wine vinegar
½ cup salad oil
2 cloves garlic, crushed
   (¼ teaspoon powdered)
¼ teaspoon freshly ground black pepper
2 teaspoons fresh basil leaves, chopped fine
   (½ teaspoon dried, crumbled)
1 teaspoon fresh marjoram leaves, chopped fine
   (¼ teaspoon dried, crumbled)
1 teaspoon fresh parsley, chopped fine
   (¼ teaspoon dried, crumbled)

Blend avocado, vinegar, oil, garlic and pepper. Stir in herbs and chill. Serve on vegetables or green salads.

Chunky Tomato Vinaigrette

Preparation time: 5 minutes
Yield: 2 cups

¼ cup red wine vinegar
½ cup salad oil
   freshly ground black pepper
   salt to taste
1 avocado, diced
2 medium tomatoes, seeded and diced
4 scallions, sliced
¼ cup fresh cilantro, stemmed
   (2 tablespoons dried, crumbled)

Blend vinegar, oil, salt and pepper. Stir in avocado, tomatoes, scallions and cilantro. Chill. Serve on vegetable salads.

Make Ahead Avocado Salads

Avocado with Lemon and Mint Sauce

Mint is a perennial herb shrub or ground cover. There are many varieties: applemint, spearmint, pennyroyal mint, watermint, black peppermint and many others. Fresh mint leaves may be used with chicken and pork dishes. Fresh or dried mint leaves may be used to make tea or boiled into a heavy syrup. Mint oil is very strong, use it sparingly.

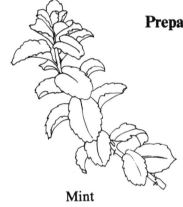

Mint

Preparation time: 15 minutes, refrigerate up to 4 hours
Yield: 4 servings

½ *cup fresh lemon juice*
1 *tablespoon fresh mint leaves, chopped*
  (¼ teaspoon dried, crumbled or 1 drop oil)
1 *teaspoon sugar*
  salt to taste
2 *avocados*

Mix lemon juice, mint, sugar and salt. Chill. Just before serving, peel and slice avocados. Pour lemon and mint mixture over avocado slices. Serve.

Apple Salad on the Half Shell

Preparation time: 15 minutes, refrigerate up to 4 hours
Yield: 4 servings

½ *cup yogurt or sour cream*
1 *tablespoon honey*
2 *apples, cored and diced (unpeeled)*
½ *cup raisins*
¼ *cup slivered almonds*
½ *cup diced celery*
2 *avocados*
4 *lettuce leaves*
  lemon juice

Mix together yogurt and honey. Toss with apples, raisins, almonds and celery. Chill. Just before serving, halve and peel avocados. Place avocado halves on lettuce lined serving dish. Sprinkle with lemon juice. Spoon apple mixture into avocado halves. Serve.

Tomatoes in Cucumber Sauce

Preparation time: 20 minutes, refrigerate up to 6 hours
Yield: 6 servings

1 medium cucumber, peeled and chopped
2 teaspoons lemon juice
½ cup sour cream or yogurt
1 tablespoon fresh dill weed, chopped
   (½ teaspoon dried, crumbled)
   salt to taste
2 large tomatoes, seeded and diced
1 small red onion, thinly sliced
3 avocados
   lemon juice
   lettuce leaves

Mix together cucumber, lemon juice, sour cream, dill and salt. Gently toss with tomatoes and onions. Chill. Just before serving, halve and peel avocados. Place halves on lettuce lined serving dish. Sprinkle with lemon juice. Spoon tomato and onion mixture into halves. Serve.

Cottage Cheese and Tomatoes

on the Half Shell

Preparation time: 10 minutes, refrigerate up to 6 hours
Yield: 4 servings

2 cups cottage cheese
2 medium tomatoes, seeded and diced
1 medium green pepper, seeded and diced
1 tablespoon fresh dill weed, chopped
   (1 teaspoon dried, crumbled)
2 avocados
   lettuce leaves
   lemon juice
   fresh dill weed

Stir together cottage cheese, tomatoes, green pepper and dill. Chill up to 6 hours. Just before serving, halve and peel avocados. Place halves on lettuce lined serving dish. Sprinkle with lemon juice. Spoon cottage cheese mixture into halves. Sprinkle with remaining dill. Serve.

Chicken and Almonds

Preparation time: 20 minutes, refrigerate up to 24 hours
Yield: 4 servings

½ cup mayonnaise (yogurt or sour cream)
2 tablespoons lemon juice
1 ½ cups diced, cooked chicken
¼ cup chopped celery
⅓ cup chopped almonds
  salt to taste
2 avocados
  lettuce
  lemon juice
1 medium tomato, chopped
4 tablespoons chopped scallions

Blend mayonnaise and lemon juice. Combine chicken, celery, almonds and salt. Toss with mayonnaise mixture until coated. Chill. Just before serving, halve and peel avocados. Place halves on lettuce lined serving dish. Sprinkle with lemon juice. Spoon chicken mixture into halves. Garnish with tomatoes and scallions. Serve.

Dilled Salmon and Cucumber Salad

Preparation time: 20 minutes, refrigerate up to 24 hours
Yield: 6 servings

2 cups canned salmon, boned and drained
⅔ cup chopped celery
½ cup chopped sweet pickles
2 tablespoons chopped onion
1 cup sour cream or yogurt
  salt to taste
¼ cup fresh dill weed
  (2 tablespoons dried, crumbled)
  freshly ground black pepper to taste
¼ teaspoon grated lemon peel
2 tablespoons lemon juice
1 cucumber, peeled and diced
3 avocados
  lettuce
  lemon juice

Stir together salmon, celery, pickles, onion, sour cream, seasonings, lemon peel and juice. Chill. Layer cucumber on lettuce leaves. Chill. Just before serving, halve and peel avocados. Place halves on cucumber. Sprinkle with lemon juice. Spoon salmon mixture into halves. Serve.

Creamy Chicken and Nectarines

Preparation time: 30 minutes, refrigerate up to 24 hours
Yield: 6 servings

1 ½ cups diced, cooked chicken
3 cups nectarines, diced
1 scallion with top, minced
2 ribs celery, chopped
¼ cup orange juice
   salt to taste
   freshly ground black pepper to taste
¼ cup whipping cream, whipped stiff
¼ cup mayonnaise (yogurt or sour cream)
3 avocados
   lettuce
   lemon juice
¼ cup chopped walnuts
   parsley

Combine chicken, nectarines, scallions, celery, orange juice, salt and pepper. Set aside. Lightly combine whipped cream and mayonnaise. Fold chicken into mixture. Chill. Just before serving, halve and peel avocados. Place halves on lettuce lined serving dish. Sprinkle with lemon juice. Spoon chicken mixture into halves. Sprinkle with chopped walnuts. Garnish with parsley. Serve.

Tomato and Green Chile Salsa

Preparation time: 20 minutes, refrigerate up to 24 hours
Yield: 6 servings

2 medium tomatoes, peeled and diced
1 green pepper, seeded and diced
1 small red onion, chopped
1 4 oz. can diced green chiles
3 tablespoons fresh cilantro, stemmed
   (1 tablespoon dried, crumbled)
3 avocados
   lettuce
   lemon juice

Toss together tomatoes, pepper, onion, chiles and cilantro. Chill. Just before serving, halve and peel avocados. Place halves on lettuce lined serving dish. Sprinkle with lemon juice. Spoon tomato mixture into halves. Serve.

Seafood and Asparagus

with Cucumber Dressing

Preparation time: 20 minutes, refrigerate up to 24 hours
Yield: 4 servings

1 *cucumber, peeled*
¼ *teaspoon celery seed*
¼ *teaspoon chili powder*
½ *cup yogurt or sour cream*
1 *cup cooked, diced seafood*
  (halibut, seabass, salmon, snapper,
  lobster, crab, shrimp or scallops)
¼ *lb. asparagus spears, cut into 1 inch*
  pieces and cooked until tender
¼ *cup chopped celery*
2 *avocados*
  lettuce
  lemon juice

Blend cucumber, celery seed, chili powder and yogurt. Toss with seafood, asparagus and celery. Chill. Just before serving, halve and peel avocados. Place halves on lettuce lined serving dish. Sprinkle with lemon juice. Spoon seafood mixture into halves. Serve.

Chili powder *found in the supermarket is a combination of dried and ground spices. Chili powder can be used for flavoring sauces, cheese dishes and vegetable soups.*

Shrimp and Watercress

Preparation time: 10 minutes, refrigerate up to 6 hours
Yield: 6 servings

½ cup mayonnaise (yogurt or sour cream)
1 teaspoon lemon juice
2 tablespoons chopped watercress
1 lb. small cooked shrimp (2 cups)
3 avocados
   lettuce leaves
   lemon juice
   watercress sprigs

Blend together mayonnaise, lemon juice and watercress. Fold in shrimp. Chill. Just before serving, halve and peel avocados. Place halves on lettuce lined serving dish. Sprinkle with lemon juice. Spoon shrimp into halves and garnish with watercress sprigs. Serve.

Tuna and Apples

Preparation time: 15 minutes, refrigerate up to 12 hours
Yield: 4 servings

½ cup mayonnaise (yogurt or sour cream)
1 teaspoon lemon juice
1 cup drained tuna
1 cup chopped apples, chilled
2 avocados
   lettuce leaves
   lemon juice

Mix mayonnaise and lemon juice. Toss with tuna and apples. Chill. Just before serving, halve and peel avocados. Place halves on lettuce leaves. Sprinkle with lemon juice. Spoon tuna mixture into halves. Serve.

Ham and Pasta

Preparation time: 20 minutes, refrigerate up to 24 hours
Yield: 6 servings

¼ cup olive oil
1 tablespoon lemon juice
¼ teaspoon dry mustard
  (1 teaspoon prepared)
¼ teaspoon paprika
1 ½ cups cooked, minced ham
½ cup chopped celery
2 scallions with tops, finely chopped
  salt to taste
  freshly ground black pepper to taste
4 cups cooked pasta*
3 avocados
  lettuce leaves
  lemon juice
12 black olives, sliced

Mix oil, lemon juice, mustard and paprika. Toss together ham, celery, scallions, salt and pepper. Toss again with pasta. Chill. Just before serving, halve and peel avocados. Place halves on lettuce lined serving dish. Spinkle with lemon juice. Spoon pasta mixture into halves. Garnish with olives. Serve.

Recipe for fresh pasta on page 85.

Shrimp Vinaigrette

Preparation: 20 minutes, refrigerate up to 6 hours
Yield: 4 servings

½ *cup chopped scallions with tops*
¼ *cup chopped fresh parsley*
1 *tablespoon chopped capers*
2 *tablespoons wine vinegar*
⅛ *teaspoon dried mustard*
   (½ teaspoon prepared mustard)
   salt to taste
   freshly ground black pepper to taste
½ *cup vegetable oil*
1 *lb. cooked large shrimp*
2 *avocados*
   lettuce leaves
   lemon juice
2 *tomatoes, cut into wedges*

Mix together scallions, parsley, capers, vinegar, mustard, salt and pepper. Gradually beat in oil until sauce thickens. Fold in shrimp. Chill. Just before serving, halve and peel avocados. Place halves on lettuce lined serving dish. Sprinkle with lemon juice. Spoon shrimp into halves. Garnish with tomato slices. Serve with any remaining dressing.

Avocado Soups

The best soups always start with homemade stock. When homemade stock is not available, bouillon cubes or canned stock may be substituted. Avocado flavors blend best and fish, chicken and beef stocks.

Chicken Stock

Preparation time: 20 minutes, plus 4 hours simmer time
Yield: 2 quarts

4 lbs. chicken parts
8 quarts water
8 whole peppercorns
1 bay leaf
5 whole cloves
5 fresh parsley sprigs
    (2 ½ tablespoons dried, crumbled)
1 medium onion, diced
3 ribs celery, diced
1 medium carrot, diced

Blanch chicken in 4 qts. boiling water for 5 minutes. Drain and discard water. Add 4 qts. water and slowly bring to boil. Lower heat. Add remaining ingredients. Simmer 4 hours. Cool uncovered.

Beef Stock

Preparation time: 15 minutes, plus 6 hours simmer time
Yield: 2 quarts

2 cups lean beef and bones
5 cups water
6 whole peppercorns
1 bay leaf
1 tablespoon fresh thyme leaves
    (1 teaspoon dried, crumbled)
3 sprigs fresh parsley
    (1 tablespoon dried, crumbled)
1 carrot, diced
2 ribs celery, diced
1 cup fresh tomatoes, peeled and
    chopped
1 medium onion, chopped

Bring all ingredients to a boil. Skim top. Lower heat. Simmer for 6 hours. Cool uncovered.

Fish Stock

Preparation time: 15 minutes, plus 15 minutes simmer time
Yield: 3 cups

3 cups water
½ cup chopped onion
¼ cup chopped carrot
½ cup chopped celery
6 whole peppercorns
2 parsley sprigs
    (1 tablespoon dried, crumbled)
3 cloves
2 tablespoons lemon juice
2 lbs. fish trimmings

Heat and simmer all ingredients uncovered for 15 minutes. Do not overcook. Strain and cool.

Chilled Avocado Yogurt Soup

Preparation time: 10 minutes, plus 20 minutes chill time
Yield: 4 servings

Chives

1   *large avocado, mashed*
½   *cup yogurt*
2   *cups chicken stock**
    salt to taste
⅛   *teaspoon white pepper*
    dash of cayenne pepper
    dash of garlic powder
1   *teaspoon chopped chives*
4   *slices of bacon, cooked and crumbled*

Blend avocado, yogurt and stock until smooth. Add salt, pepper, cayenne and garlic powder, blend again. Sprinkle with chopped chives and bacon. Chill.

***Chives** are grass-like herbs with hollow stems. They have a mild onion flavor. Chives are excellent in soups, omelettes, salads and fish dishes. Chives do not keep well dried or frozen. Scallions may be used if chives are not available.*

*Please read about stocks on page 73.

Cucumber, Tomato and Avocado Soup

Preparation time: 10 minutes, plus 20 minutes chill time
Yield: 4 servings

1 *avocado, mashed*
2 *cups chicken stock**
½ *cup sour cream or yogurt*
1 *tablespoon lemon juice*
  salt to taste
  dash cayenne pepper
1 *large tomato, seeded and diced*
1 *cucumber, peeled and*
  diced into bite size pieces
2 *tablespoons bacon bits*

Blend avocado with stock, sour cream, lemon juice, salt and cayenne pepper. Stir cucumbers and tomatoes into soup. Garnish with bacon bits. Chill.

Watercress and Avocado Soup

Preparation time: 10 minutes, plus 20 minutes chill time
Yield: 4 servings

2 *avocados, mashed*
3 *tablespoons chopped onion*
2 *cups watercress sprigs*
1½ *cups chicken stock**
1 *cup half and half*
  salt to taste
2 *teaspoons lemon juice*
  watercress sprigs

Blend avocado with onion until smooth. Add watercress and stock. Blend until watercress is finely chopped. Add half and half, salt and lemon juice. Blend. Garnish with extra sprigs of watercress. Chill.

Please read about stocks on page 73.

Avocado Soup with Garlic

Preparation time: 10 minutes, plus 20 minutes chill time
Yield: 4 servings

3 *avocados, mashed*
2 *large cloves garlic, crushed*
1½ *cups chicken stock**
2 *teaspoons lime juice*
salt to taste
1½ *cups half and half*
lime slices
sour cream or yogurt

Garlic

Blend avocados with garlic, stock, lime juice and salt. Add half and half. Blend. Pour into serving dish and garnish with slices of lime and sour cream. Chill.

Chunky Chicken and Avocado Soup

Preparation time: 10 minutes
Yield: 4 servings

½ *cup chopped onion*
1 *clove garlic, crushed*
2 *tablespoons butter*
4 *cups chicken stock**
1½ *cups diced, cooked chicken*
½ *cup canned mild enchilada sauce*
1 *avocado, diced and chilled*

Sauté onion and garlic in butter until tender. Add stock, chicken and enchilada sauce. Simmer for 15 minutes. Cool slightly, then add chilled avocado cubes. Serve.

*Please read about stocks on page 73.

Hot Cream Soup with Chicken

Preparation time: 20 minutes
Yield: 6 servings

1 can (10 oz.) cream of chicken soup
1 can (10 oz.) cream of celery soup
¾ cup half and half
2 cups milk
  salt to taste
  freshly ground black pepper to taste
½ bay leaf
1 cup diced, cooked chicken
1 avocado, diced
½ cup pitted black olives, sliced

Bay

Stir together soups, half and half, milk, salt, pepper and bay leaf in a sauce pan. Add chicken and olives. Heat through. Remove bay leaf. Stir in avocado. Serve.

Bay is an evergreen tree or shrub, with long and oval leaves. It has a leathery texture and is very aromatic. These leaves are flavor enhancers for broth, soups and stews.

Avocado Seafood Bisque

Preparation time: 30 minutes
Yield:H 4 servings

½ lb. bacon
⅓ cup finely chopped onions
⅓ cup finely chopped celery
1 medium potato, peeled and diced
4 cups fish stock*
1 bay leaf
2 sprigs fresh parsley
* (2 teaspoons dried, crumbled)*
2 teaspoons fresh thyme leaves
* (½ teaspoon dried, crumbled)*
1½ lbs. cooked seafood
* (halibut, seabass, salmon, snapper,*
* lobster, crab, shrimp or scollops)*
1½ cups half and half
¼ cup dry white wine
2 avocados, diced

Cook bacon until crisp. Remove from pan and drain on paper towel. Sauté onion and celery in bacon fat. Stir in fish stock. Add potato. Tie fresh herbs in muslin bag (dried herbs may be added directly to stock). Add to fish stock. Cook over low heat for 15 minutes. Add seafood. Cook 5 to 6 minutes. Remove from heat. Remove spice bag. Stir in cream, wine and avocado. Reheat gently. Serve.

*Please read about stocks on page 73.

Avocado Sauces

Hollandaise Sauce

Preparation time: 10 minutes
Yield: 2 cups

2 eggs
¼ cup lemon juice
½ cup butter, melted and bubbly hot
1 avocados, mashed
1 teaspoon finely chopped onion
  dash of cayenne pepper
  salt to taste

Place eggs and lemon juice in blender. Mix at high speed until light yellow in color. Lower blender speed and add remaining ingredients until well blended. Heat in a double boiler until heated through. Serve as a sauce for eggs, toast or artichokes.

Tomato and Onion Salsa

Preparation time: 10 minutes
Yield: 2 cups

2 avocados, coarsely chopped
2 tomatoes, coarsely chopped
1 medium onion, coarsely chopped
2 cloves garlic, crushed
1 small bell pepper, coarsely chopped
¼ cup fresh cilantro leaves
  (2 tablespoons dried, crumbled)
1 (4 oz.) can diced green chiles

Toss together all ingredients. Chill. Serve with chips or on salads, eggs, tacos, chicken dishes or baked potatoes.

Creamy Mushroom Sauce

Preparation time: 15 minutes
Yield: 2 ½ cups

½ cup finely chopped onion
¼ cup finely chopped celery
1 clove garlic, crushed
½ cup sliced mushrooms
½ cup butter
2 tablespoons flour
½ teaspoon white pepper
½ cup chicken stock*
1½ cups grated cheese
½ cup white wine
1 avocado, mashed

Sauté onion, celery, garlic and mushrooms in butter over medium heat. Lower heat and stir in flour and pepper. Add chicken stock and bring to a boil. Remove from heat and stir in cheese, wine and avocado. Serve with chicken or egg dishes.

Creamed Horseradish Sauce

Horseradish is a large weedy looking plant that is grown for its roots. The roots are grated or creamed and mixed with vinegar or cream to make condiments.

Preparation time: 10 minutes
Yield: 2 cups

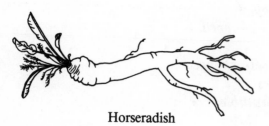

Horseradish

¼ cup finely chopped onion
2 tablespoons butter
1 tablespoon flour
1 cup fish stock
½ cup sour cream or yogurt
1 tablespoon prepared horseradish
1 avocado, diced

Sauté onion in butter over medium heat. Lower heat and stir in flour. Add fish stock. Cook until the sauce begins to thicken. Remove from heat and stir in sour cream, horseradish and avocado. Serve with seafood.

*Please read about stock on page 73.

Avocado Entrées

Lemon and Avocado Pasta

Preparation time: 25 minutes, plus 1 hour standing time
Yield: 4 servings

¼ *cup lemon juice*
½ *cup salad oil*
½ *teaspoon paprika*
salt to taste
1 *clove garlic, crushed*
¼ *cup minced parsley*
½ *lb. mushrooms, sliced*
1 *avocado, sliced*

Blend lemon juice, oil, paprika, salt, garlic and parsley. Toss with mushrooms and avocado. Chill.

Fresh pasta

1⅓ *cups flour*
2 *eggs, lightly beaten*
2 *tablespoons water*
2 *teaspoons cooking oil*

Mix eggs, flour, water and oil with a fork. Fold mixture with hands until dough pulls free from hands. Add more flour if necessary. Knead 10 minutes. Cover and let stand 1 hour. Roll and stretch dough until thin and translucent. Let stand 10 minutes. Before dough becomes brittle, roll it into a scroll and slice on bias into ¼ inch thick noodles. Drop noodles into rapidly boiling water for about 5 minutes. Do not overcook. Drain thoroughly. Toss with lemon mixture, mushroom and avocado mixture. Serve.

Cheesy Tomato and Avocado Pizza

Preparation time: 20 minutes, 2 hours rising time, 15 minutes bake time
Yield: 1 pizza

Dough

    1 cake yeast
    1⅓ cup water
    4 cups sifted flour
    2 tablespoons salad oil
    salt to taste

Soften yeast in water. Add flour, oil and salt. Mix thoroughly. Turn onto floured board and knead for 10 minutes. Let rise for 2 hours.

Sauce

    1 can (28 oz.) Italian tomatoes, strained
    ½ cup tomato paste
    2 tablespoons finely grated onion
    ½ teaspoon sugar
    1 ½ teaspoon fresh basil leaves, chopped
       (½ teaspoon dried, crumbled)

Combine all ingredients in sauce pan. Bring to a boil, lower heat and simmer for 15 to 20 minutes.

Topping

    4 cups shredded mozzarella cheese
    2 large tomatoes, sliced
    2 large avocados, sliced
    1 medium red onion, sliced
       oregano
    6 black olives, sliced

Preheat oven to 500 degrees. Punch dough down and spread over pizza pan or cookie sheet. Form a rim around outer edge. Place a thin layer of cheese on dough. Spread sauce over dough, top with remaining cheese, tomato slices, avocado slices and onion. Sprinkle with oregano and black olives. Bake for 15 minutes. Serve piping hot.

Cream Cheese and Avocado Omelette

Preparation time: 15 minutes
Yield: 2 servings

  4 eggs
¼ cup milk
  salt to taste
  dash white pepper
⅛ teaspoon paprika
1½ tablespoons butter
  1 avocado, sliced
  2 oz. cream cheese, softened
  chopped chives

Beat eggs, milk, salt, pepper and paprika together. Melt butter in a large skillet over medium heat. Tilt pan to coat all sides evenly. Pour egg mixture into pan, tilt to permit uncooked egg to run to sides and bottom. Stick egg with a fork to let heat through. Lower heat and cook 2 to 3 minutes or until egg is slighty firm through. Spoon or drop cream cheese across the center of eggs. Top with avocado slices and roll the edges of egg over filling. Remove from heat and cover for 2 to 3 minutes or until cheese is melted. Sprinkle with chopped chives. Serve hot.

Paprika *is dried and ground sweet red pepper. It has a very mild flavor and is used widely for its decorative quality.*

Avocado Soufflé

When preparing a soufflé, preheat the oven well in advance. Beat egg white in stainless steel or copper bowls, glass bowls won't allow the egg to stick and climb the sides. Aluminum bowls may discolor the egg whites. Prepare the mold carefully with butter and dusting cheese (as the cheese melts, the soufflé expands up the side of the dish). The soufflé must always be kept away from drafts and served at once in the oven-proof, straight-sided dish in which it is cooked. Follow the instructions carefully to insure a perfect soufflé.

Preheat oven: 350 degrees
Preparation time: 20 minutes, plus 35 minutes bake time
Yield: 4 servings

3 tablespoons butter
¼ cup grated parmesan cheese
2 tablespoons flour
1 cup milk
½ cup grated cheddar cheese
⅛ teaspoon dry mustard
   (½ teaspoon prepared)
⅛ teaspoon cayenne pepper
   salt and pepper to taste
4 eggs, separated
1 avocado, mashed

With 1 tablespoon of butter, grease bottom and sides of 8 inch soufflé dish. Dust with dry cheese. Melt remaining butter in sauce pan. Stir in flour. Cook over low heat, stirring constantly. Stir in milk, cheese, mustard, cayenne, salt and pepper. Remove from heat and add beaten egg yolks. Combine with avocado pulp and set aside. Beat egg whites until stiff, but not dry. Gently fold egg whites into avocado mixture. Pour into soufflé dish. Bake at 350 degrees for 35 minutes. Serve at once.

Avocado Tacos

Preparation time: 15 minutes
Yield: 12 tacos

3 *avocados, mashed*
½ *teaspoon cayenne pepper*
2 *tablespoons sour cream*
  salt to taste
10 *black olives, chopped*
1 *tablespoon cilantro, stemmed*
12 *corn tortillas*
  cooking oil
1½ *cups shredded lettuce*
1½ *cups grated cheddar cheese*

Blend avocado, cayenne, sour cream and salt until smooth. Stir in chopped olives and cilantro. Cook tortillas on both sides on a hot, lightly oiled griddle. Spoon avocado mixture onto tortillas and fold over. Top with lettuce and cheese. Serve.

Cayenne is dried, ground, very hot, red pepper. Used sparingly, it will make a wonderful addition to sauces, dips, salad dressings, eggs and poultry.

Crispy Fried Avocado Cups

with Spicy Meat Filling

Preparation time: 45 minutes
Yield: 6 servings

Filling

>   1 lb. shredded beef or pork
>   1 4 oz. can diced green chiles
>   ½ cup mild enchilada sauce
>   ¼ minced onion
>   1 clove garlic, crushed

Sauté meat, onion and garlic until lightly browned. Drain excess fat. Stir in chiles and enchilada sauce. Simmer until filling thickens to a paste.

Sauce

>   1 cup beef stock
>   1 cup tomato sauce
>   ⅛ teaspoon ground cinnamon
>   ⅛ teaspoon ground cloves
>   ⅛ teaspoon ground cumin
>   ¼ teaspoon pepper
>   ½ teaspoon salt
>   1 tablespoon capers
>   1 tablespoon chopped fresh parsley
>   (1 teaspoon dried, crumbled)
>   cooking oil
>   3 large avocados halved and peeled
>   3 eggs, beaten
>   1 tablespoon flour

Stir together all ingredients in a saucepan. Simmer for 20 to 30 minutes. Pour sauce into a large baking dish and place it in the oven on low heat to keep warm. Heat 1 inch oil in a large skillet. Slightly enlarge the cavity of the avocado halves. Fill halves with meat mixture. Pack it firmly, forming a mound. Sprinkle with flour and pat with hands to coat evenly. Dip avocado halves in beaten egg and roll until evenly coated. Place avocado halves in hot oil, filling side down until lightly browned. Carefully turn avocados over and roll to brown the rounded sides. Remove from oil and drain on paper towel. Place avocados in tomato sauce and serve.

Chicken Breasts in Creamy Avocado Sauce

Preheat oven: 350 degrees
Preparation time: 20 minutes, plus 15 minutes bake time
Yield: 4 servings

4 *chicken breast halves, skinned and boned*
salt to taste
freshly ground black pepper to taste
flour
½ *cup butter*
½ *cup chopped onion*
¼ *cup chopped celery*
1 *clove garlic*
½ *lb. mushrooms*
2 *tablespoons flour*
½ *teaspoon white pepper*
½ *cup white wine*
½ *cup chicken stock**
1½ *cups grated cheddar cheese*
1 *avocado, mashed*

Pound chicken breasts until flat and tender. Dredge with salt, pepper and flour. Melt ¼ cup of butter in large skillet. Saute chicken breasts until evenly browned on both sides. Remove from skillet and set aside. Place remaining butter in skillet. Saute onion, celery, garlic and mushrooms until tender. Slowly add flour, then stock. Cook until thick. Stir in wine, avocado and cheese. Heat through. Place chicken breasts in baking dish, pour sauce over. Bake at 350 degrees for 15 minutes. Serve hot.

*Please read about stocks on page 73.

Curried Chicken with Chopped Peanuts

Preheat oven: 350 degrees
Preparation time: 25 minutes, plus 10 minutes bake time
Yield: 6 servings

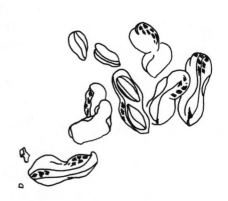

¼ cup butter
½ cup chopped, pared apple
¼ cup chopped onion
1 clove garlic, crushed
1 tablespoon curry powder
¼ cup flour
1 cup half and half
1 cup chicken stock*
salt to taste
black pepper to taste
2 cups cooked diced chicken
3 avocados, sliced
3 cups cooked rice
¼ cup chopped peanuts

Melt butter over medium high heat. Sauté apple, onion, garlic and curry powder until onion is translucent. Stir in flour. Gradually add cream and broth. Reduce heat. Cook and stir until sauce boils. Add salt, pepper and chicken. Cook over low heat for 10 minutes. Place avocado slices on rice in baking dish. Heat in 350 degree oven for 5 minutes. Spoon hot curried chicken over avocado slices. Sprinkle chopped peanuts over chicken and serve.

*Please read about stocks on page 73.

Teriyaki Chicken and Avocados

Preparation time: 15 minutes, plus 2 hours marinating time, 30 minutes bake time
Yield: 6 servings

⅛ *cup sesame oil*
⅛ *cup vegetable oil*
½ *cup soy sauce*
1 *tablespoon brown sugar*
1 *clove garlic, crushed*
1 *teaspoon grated fresh ginger*
   (¼ teaspoon dried, ground)
1 *tablespoon dry sherry*
3 *whole chicken breasts, boned*
3 *cups cooked brown rice*
2 *avocados, diced*

Mix oil, soy sauce, sugar, garlic, ginger and sherry. Pour over chicken and marinate for 2 hours. Bake uncovered at 375 degrees for 30 minutes. Layer serving dish with rice and avocados. Top with baked chicken. Pour remaining sauce over entire dish and serve.

Honey Orange Glazed Chicken

Preheat oven: 375 degrees
Preparation time: 20 minutes, plus 45 minutes bake time
Yield: 4 servings

1 (3 lb.) chicken, cut in half
salt to taste
pepper to taste
flour
3 tablespoons butter
1 large onion, chopped
¼ cup orange juice
¼ cup chicken stock
3 tablespoons orange marmalade
1 teaspoon paprika
salt and pepper to taste
1 orange, sliced
3 avocados, sliced
juice of 1 lemon

Dredge chicken in salt, pepper and flour. Melt butter in large skillet. Brown chicken halves on all sides. Remove chicken from skillet and set aside. Sauté onion in remaining butter. Combine orange juice, chicken stock and marmalade. Pour ½ mixture into skillet. Set aside. Place chicken in baking dish, sprinkle with paprika, salt and pepper. Spoon remaining orange mixture over chicken. Bake at 375 degrees uncovered for 10 minutes. Place orange slices on chicken, cover and bake 35 minutes longer (or until chicken pulls apart easily). Baste chicken frequently with the juice from the baking dish. Place avocado slices on serving dish. Sprinkle with lemon juice. Place baked chicken halves on avocado slices. Pour remaining sauce over and serve.

*Please read about stocks on page 73.

Avocado Turkey Newburg

Preparation time: 35 minutes
Yield: 4 servings

1 teaspoon chopped onion
2 tablespoons butter
¾ cup half and half
2 egg yolks, beaten
½ cup butter, melted
¼ cup dry sherry
1½ cups diced, cooked turkey
2 avocados, diced
8 pieces toast

Cook onion and 2 tablespoons butter over low heat for 5 minutes. Place in a double boiler. Beat half and half and egg yolks together. Stir in melted butter. Do not boil, sauce may curdle. Add sherry, turkey and avocado. Heat through. Serve on toast.

Seafood Curry

Preparation time: 20 minutes, plus 1 hour cooking time
Yield: 4 servings

2 *tablespoons butter*
2 *tablespoons flour*
2 *cups fish stock*
¼ *cup mushroom gratings*
  (about 8 mushrooms grated in blender)
¾ *cup chicken stock*
1 *egg yolk (beaten with 2 tablespoons cream)*
1 *teaspoon curry powder*
2 *cups diced cooked seafood*
  (halibut, seabass, salmon, snapper,
  lobster, crab, shrimp or scallops)
  juice of 1 lemon
2 *avocados, halved and peeled*

Melt butter in double boiler. Stir in flour. Slowly add fish stock and mushrooms. Cook over medium heat for 1 hour. Stir in chicken stock. Remove from heat. Add egg yolk, curry and seafood. Heat through. Do not boil, sauce may curdle. Sprinkle lemon juice over avocado halves. Spoon seafood mixture into avocado halves and serve.

Please read about stocks on page 73.

Shrimp and Scallop Sauté

Preparation time: 25 minutes
Yield: 4 servings

2 tablespoons butter
½ lb. medium shrimp
½ lb. baby scallops
1 large clove garlic, minced
2 avocados, sliced
3 tablespoons lemon juice
½ cup shredded cheddar cheese
¼ cup seasoned bread crumbs

Melt butter in large skillet. Sauté shrimp, scallops and garlic in butter until tender (about five minutes). Do not overcook. Layer avocado slices in baking dish and sprinkle with lemon juice. Pour seafood mixture over avocados. Top with shredded cheese and bread crumbs. Broil 3 to 4 minutes or until cheese is melted and browned. Serve.

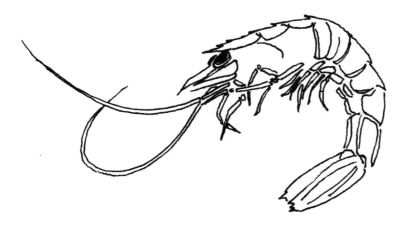

Creamed Seafood and Avocado

Preparation time: 20 minutes
Yield: 4 servings

2 tablespoons butter
1½ tablespoons flour
1 cup milk
1 cup fish stock
  celery salt
  dash nutmeg
1 teaspoon lemon juice
½ teaspoon Worcestershire sauce
1 teaspoon onion juice
2 teaspoons fresh parsley, chopped
  (½ teaspoon dried, crumbled)
2 teaspoons chopped chives
2 cups cooked, diced seafood
  (halibut, seabass, salmon, snapper,
  lobster, crab, shrimp or scallops)
2 teaspoons dry sherry
2 avocados, sliced
  fresh parsley
  orange slices

Melt butter over low heat. Stir in flour with a wire whisk, stirring continuously 3 to 4 minutes. Slowly add milk, then fish stock. Stir in celery salt, nutmeg, lemon juice, Worcestershire sauce, onion, parsley and chives. Simmer until sauce thickens. Fold in seafood and heat through. Stir in sherry and pour over avocado slices. Garnish with parsley and orange slices.

*Please read about stocks on page 73.

Red Snapper Fillets

with Cream of Avocado Sauce

Preparation time: 15 minutes, plus 1 hour marinating time
Yield: 4 servings

4 red snapper fillets
1 cup white wine
2 tablespoons butter
2 teaspoons paprika

Marinate fillets in wine for 1 hour. Drain on paper towel. Butter both sides of fillets. Sprinkle with paprika. Grill fillets 4 to 5 minutes each side or until fish flakes easily. Spoon sauce over fillets. Serve with lemon wedges.

Cream of Avocado Sauce

2 tablespoons butter
2 tablespoons onion, finely chopped
2 tablespoons flour
½ teaspoon salt
1 cup water
½ cup sour cream
2 teaspoons horseradish
1 avocado, diced

Sauté onion in butter until tender. Stir in flour and salt. Slowly stir in water. Boil for 1 minute. Remove from heat, stir in sour cream, horseradish and avocado. Heat gently.

A rule of thumb for cooking fish is to measure the thickest part of the fish and cook it 10 minutes (total) for every inch thick.

Sizzling Shark Kabobs

with Avocado Butter

Shark meat is moist and delicate without a fishy flavor. Freeze it if it is not to be eaten right away. Halibut or swordfish may be substituted in recipes calling for shark.

Preparation time: 15 minutes, plus 1 hour marinating time
Yield: 4 servings

1½ lb. shark steak, cut into 1 inch cubes
2 cups barbecue sauce
8 wooden skewers

Skewer shark cubes. Marinate in barbecue sauce for 2 hours. Broil or barbecue kabobs for 10 minutes, rotating to cook evenly. Serve with Avocado Butter and lemon wedges.

Avocado Butter

½ cup butter, softened
1 avocado, mashed
4 tablespoons lemon juice
2 tablespoons chopped parsley
1 teaspoon Worcestershire sauce
1 small clove garlic, crushed

Blend all ingredients together. Chill.

Steak Tostadas

with Avocado Salsa

Preparation time: 35 minutes, plus 2 hours marinating time
Yield: 4 servings

¼ cup water
3 tablespoons Dijon style mustard
  (1 tablespoon dried, ground mustard)
2 tablespoons cooking oil
1 tablespoon soy sauce
2 lbs. round steak
8 corn tortillas, cooked crisp
2 cups sour cream

Combine for marinade: water, mustard, oil and soy sauce. Score meat on both sides and marinate for 2 hours, turning frequently. Drain meat, reserving marinade. Grill or broil meat to taste. Baste while cooking. Carve meat into strips and place on tortillas. Spoon remaining marinade over. Top with avocado Salsa and sour cream.

Avocado Salsa

1 avocado, diced
1 tomato, diced
1 4 oz. can green chiles
1 tablespoon sliced scallion
1 tablespoon cilantro, stemmed
½ teaspoon cumin seed
  salt to taste

Toss together all ingredients. Chill.

Lemon Veal with Avocados

Preparation time: 35 minutes
Yield: 4 servings

5 to 6 *veal scallops (about 1 lb.) cut ⅛ inch thick*
1 *egg, beaten*
2 *tablespoons flour*
3 *tablespoons butter*
1 *tablespoon cooking oil*
¼ *cup vermouth*
½ *cup chicken stock*
3 *tablespoons lemon juice*
salt to taste
½ *teaspoon pepper*
¼ *cup chopped parsley*
1 *avocado, sliced*
juice of one lemon

Soak veal in egg for 1 hour. Remove from egg and roll in flour, coating evenly. Melt butter and oil in large skillet on medium heat. Sauté veal for 3 minutes each side or until lightly browned. Add vermouth, broth, lemon juice, salt and pepper. Stir gently until sauce becomes creamy. Cover and simmer for 10 minutes. Add parsley, simmer for 5 minutes more. Place avocado on serving dish and sprinkle with lemon juice. Place veal on avocado slices. Pour remaining sauce over. Serve.

Parsley is an herb of finely cut, fully tufted dark green leaves. It has a sweet pungency and is used fresh or dried. Parsley has traditionally been used as a garnish, but should also be considered a primary ingredient in soups, stews and casseroles. Fresh parsley will retain its flavor if dried or frozen. It takes a little more drying time than other herbs because of its dense leaves.

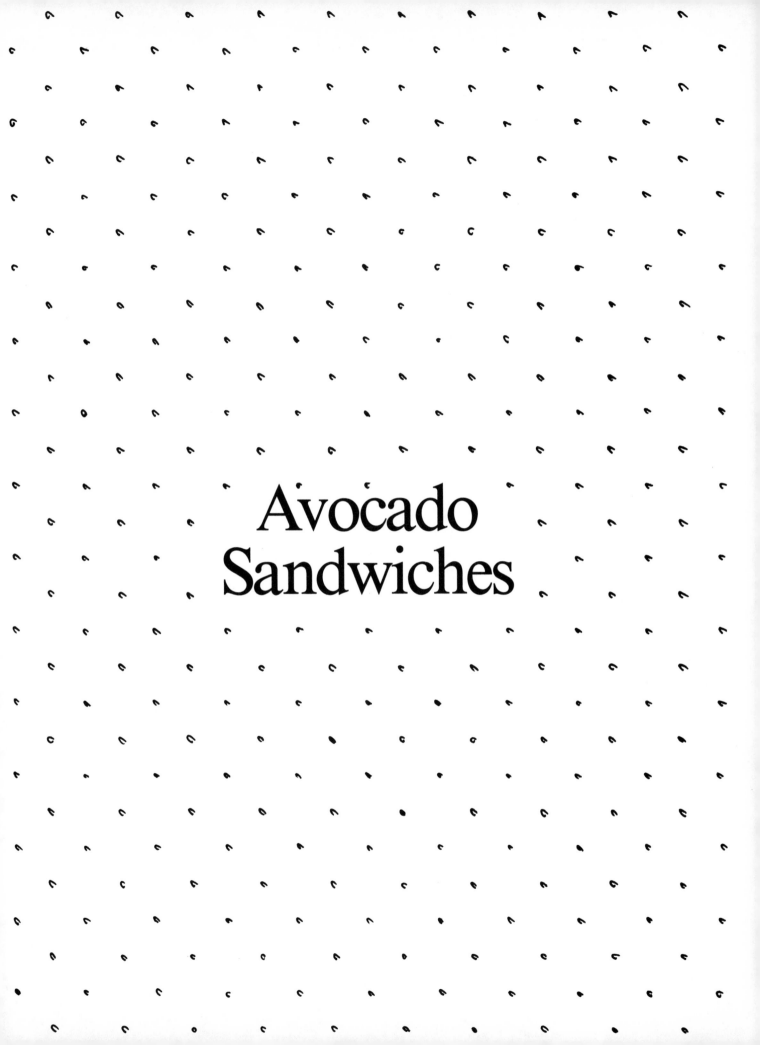

Avocado
Sandwiches

Turkey and Herb Croissants

Preparation time: 10 minutes
Yield: 4 sandwiches

1 avocado, mashed
¼ cup butter, softened
1 tablespoon lemon juice
2 tablespoons fresh herbs
(2 teaspoons dried, crumbled) parsley, chervil,
chives, basil, marjoram, oregano, or tarragon
4 croissants, sliced lengthwise
4 slices turkey
4 slices swiss cheese
4 tomato slices
4 scallions

Blend avocado, butter, lemon juice and herbs until smooth. Spoon mixture onto croissants. Layer with turkey, cheese and tomatoes. Serve with scallions.

Avocado, Swiss Cheese and Onion Sandwich

Preparation time: 10 minutes
Yield: 4 sandwiches

⅓ cup mayonnaise
2 tablespoons prepared mustard
8 slices whole wheat toast
2 avocados, sliced
4 slices Swiss cheese
4 thin slices sweet red onion
4 lettuce leaves

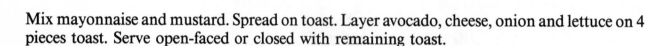

Mix mayonnaise and mustard. Spread on toast. Layer avocado, cheese, onion and lettuce on 4 pieces toast. Serve open-faced or closed with remaining toast.

Spring Garden Sandwich

Preparation time: 10 minutes
Yield: 4 sandwiches

½ cup raisins
½ cup grated carrots
2 tablespoons chopped scallions
⅛ cup shelled sunflower seeds
¼ cup mayonnaise
dash of black pepper
8 slices fresh, soft pumpernickel bread
2 avocados, sliced

Mix raisins, carrots, scallions, seeds, mayonnaise and pepper. Spread mixture onto 4 slices of bread, top with avocado and remaining bread. Serve.

Avocado, Bacon and Tomato Sandwiches

Preparation time: 10 minutes
Yield: 4 sandwiches

⅓ cup mayonnaise
1 tablespoon lemon juice
8 slices whole wheat bread, toasted
2 avocados, sliced
8 slices bacon, halved and cooked crisp
2 tomatoes, sliced

Blend mayonnaise with lemon juice and spread on toast. Top with avocado, bacon and tomato. Serve.

Ham and Homemade Slaw Sandwiches

Preparation time: 10 minutes
Yield: 4 sandwiches

2 cups shredded cabbage
¼ cup grated carrot
½ cup blue cheese dressing (below)
½ teaspoon celery seed
8 slices whole wheat bread
4 slices baked ham
2 avocados, sliced
4 lettuce leaves

Combine cabbage, carrots, dressing and celery seed. Spread cabbage mixture generously onto 4 slices of bread. Layer with baked ham, avocado and lettuce leaves. Top with remaining bread and serve.

Blue Cheese Dressing

½ cup crumbled blue cheese
⅓ cup oil
2 tablespoons vinegar
2 tablespoons water

Blend all ingredients. Chill.

Shrimp and Blue Cheese with Watercress Dressing

Preparation time: 10 minutes
Yield: 4 sandwiches

4 lettuce leaves
2 avocados, sliced
1 lb. cooked, cleaned shrimp
¼ lb. blue cheese, crumbled

1 cup sour cream
⅓ cup chopped watercress
4 tablespoons fresh dill weed
  (1½ teaspoons dried, crumbled)
1 teaspoon lemon juice
4 slices rye or pumpernickel bread

Top bread with lettuce, avocado, shrimp and blue cheese. Mix sour cream, watercress, dill and lemon juice. Generously spoon over sandwiches and serve.

Open-Faced Seafood Sandwich

Preparation time: 10 minutes
Yield: 4 sandwiches

¼ cup mayonnaise
1 tablespoon lemon juice
2 tablespoons fresh dill weed
  (½ teaspoon dried, crumbled)
  freshly ground black pepper
1 cup cooked seafood, broken into pieces
4 slices sour dough bread, toasted
2 avocados, sliced

Mix mayonnaise, lemon juice, dill and pepper. Fold in seafood. Layer avocado on toast. Spoon seafood mixture over avocado. Serve.

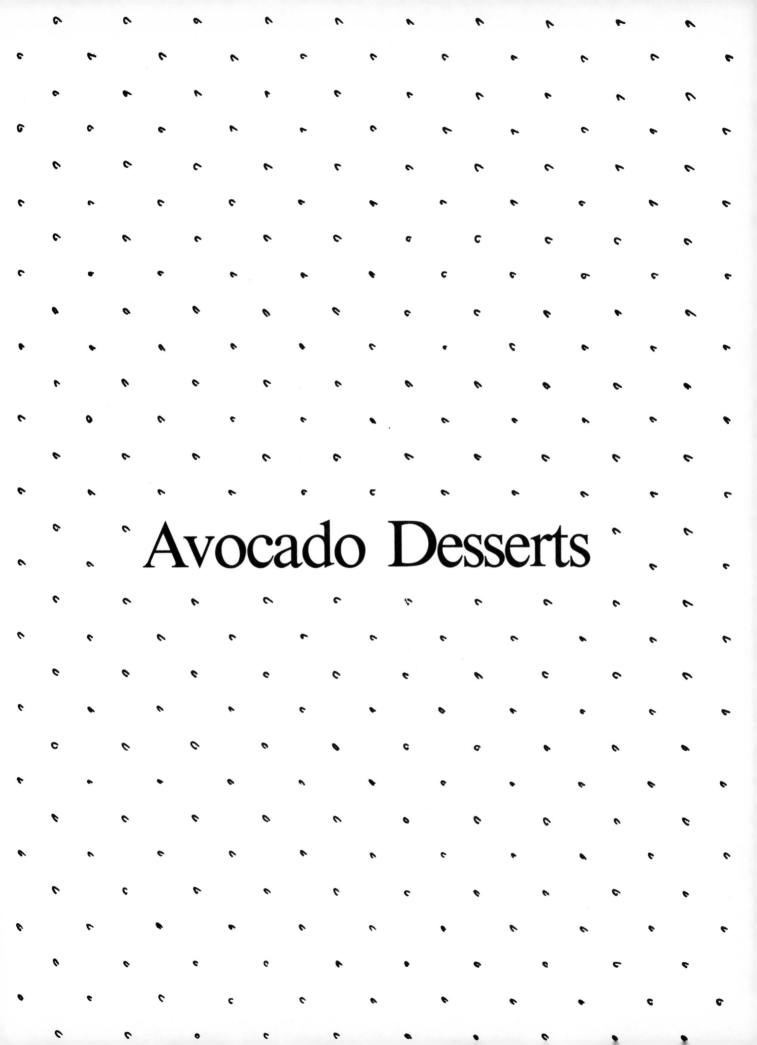

Avocado Desserts

Avocado
Ice Cream

Preparation time: 45 minutes, plus 2 hours chilling time
Pack churn with rock salt and ice.
(layer ice and rock salt 3 to 1)
Yield: 1½ quarts

3 cups milk, scalded
4 eggs, beaten
2 cups sugar
  dash of salt
1 tablespoon vanilla extract
3 cups whipping cream
8 avocados (about 7 cups), mashed
1 cup pistachio nuts

Place cooled, scalded milk in double boiler. Mix eggs, sugar and salt. Add to milk. Cook, stirring constantly, until mixture coats spoon. Pour into bowl. Add cream, vanilla and avocados. Pour into freezing container until ⅔ full. Let stand 3 minutes before churning. Churn slowly, about 40 revolutions per minute, until a slight pull develops. Churn about 120 revolutions per minute for 5 to 6 minutes. Repack freezer with ice and salt. Add pistachio nuts. Churn at 80 revolutions for a few minutes. Cover churn with burlap or newspapers. Let stand 2 hours. Serve.

Avocado Cranberry Sherbert

Preparation time: 15 minutes, plus 2 hours chilling time
Yield: 4 servings

2 *teaspoons unflavored gelatin*
1 *cup cold water*
1 *cup cranberry juice*
1 *cup sugar*
  dash of salt
2 *tablespoons lemon juice*
2 *avocados*

Combine gelatin and water in a sauce pan. Heat slowly until gelatin dissolves. Add cranberry juice, sugar, salt and lemon juice. Bring to a boil. Pour mixture into a freezing dish. Freeze 1 hour. Dice avocado and stir into partially frozen gelatin mixture. Freeze 1 hour more. Serve.

Avocado Banana Split

Preparation time: 5 minutes
Yield: 4 servings

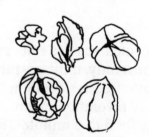

4 *bananas, peeled*
2 *avocados, quartered*
1 *pint vanilla ice cream*
½ *cup chopped walnuts*

Split bananas and lay in serving dishes. Arrange avocados around bananas. Scoop ice cream onto centers. Top with nuts and serve.

Avocado Lime Cream Pie

Preparation time: 10 minutes, plus 1 hour chilling time
Yield: 2 pies

6 avocados, mashed
¼ cup lime juice
1 10 oz. can condensed milk
3 cups whipping cream
2 graham cracker crusts*

Blend avocados, lime juice and condensed milk until smooth. Pour into crusts. Chill for 1 hour. Whip cream. Spoon onto pie. Serve.

Avocado Popsicles

Preparation time: 5 minutes, plus 2 hours freezing time
Yield: 10 popsicles

2 avocados, mashed
4 tablespoons lemon juice
10 popsicle sticks

Blend avocados and lemon juice until smooth. Pour into ice cube trays and freeze. When partially set, insert sticks. Freeze until firm.

*Recipe for graham cracker crust on page 115.

Chilled Avocado Soufflé

Preparation time: 20 minutes, plus 2 hours chilling time
Yield: 6 servings

2 avocados, mashed
¼ cup lime juice
1 envelope unflavored gelatin
¾ cup sugar
⅛ teaspoon salt
4 eggs, separated
¼ cup water
3 tablespoons light rum
1 cup whipping cream, whipped stiff
Rum Cream, given below

Blend avocado and lime juice, set aside. In top of double boiler combine gelatin, ½ cup sugar and salt. Beat egg yolks with water, add to gelatin. Stir over boiling water until gelatin is dissolved, about 5 minutes. Remove from heat. Stir in rum and avocado. Cool until mixture mounds slightly when dropped from a spoon. Beat egg whites until foamy, gradually beat in remaining sugar until stiff but not dry. Fold with whipped cream into gelatin mixture. Pour into 1 quart soufflé dish. Chill until firm. Serve with Rum Cream.

Rum Cream

½ cup whipping cream
1 tablespoon light rum

Whip ingredients together until stiff. Spoon over avocado Soufflé.

Avocado Cheesecake

Preheat oven: 350 degrees
Preparation time: 35 minutes
Yield: 1 pie

Graham Cracker Crust

3 cups graham cracker crumbs
½ cup confectioners sugar
½ cup butter, melted
1 teaspoon cinnamon

Stir together crumbs, sugar, butter and cinnamon. Spread all but ½ cup mixture into pie pan. Bake 10 minutes at 350 degrees. Cool.

Filling

4 eggs, separated, yolks beaten
¾ cup sugar
⅓ cup milk
2 tablespoons gelatin
½ cup water
2 teaspoons vanilla
16 oz. cream cheese
2 avocados, mashed
½ cup sugar

Heat in top of double boiler: beaten egg yolks, sugar and milk, until sugar dissolves. Mix gelatin and water. Add to milk mixture. Stir in vanilla. Beat together cream cheese and avocado. Stir into milk mixture. Beat egg whites until stiff (not dry). Slowly add sugar. Beat until stiff. Fold avocado mixture into egg whites. Pour mixture in crusts. Chill.

Strawberry Glazed Avocado Cups

Preparation time: 35 minutes
Yield: 4 servings

Glaze

>   2 **tablespoons unflavored gelatin**
>   ¼ **cup lemon juice**
>   1 **tablespoon corn syrup**

In top of double boiler, combine gelatin, lemon juice and corn syrup. Cook until gelatin is dissolved. Cook over low heat for 3 minutes. Remove from heat. Set aside.

Filling

>   2 **avocados, diced, shells retained**
>   ½ **grapefruit, peeled and sectioned**
>   1 **cup fresh strawberries**
>   1 **tablespoon lemon juice**
>   1 **tablespoon corn syrup**

Gently toss avocados, grapefruit and strawberries. Blend lemon juice and corn syrup, pour over fruit mixture and toss again. Fill shells with fruit. Spoon glaze over fruit. Chill.

Topping

>   ¼ **cup salad oil**
>   2 **tablespoons corn syrup**
>   2 **tablespoons lemon juice**
>   ⅛ **teaspoon salt**
>   1 **teaspoon sugar**
>   1 **teaspoon flour**
>   1 **egg, separated**

Combine oil, syrup, lemon juice, salt, sugar, flour and egg yolk. Beat thoroughly. Cook in top of double boiler until thick, stirring constantly. Beat egg white until firm, fold into cooked mixture and cool. Spoon onto fruit just before serving.

Avocado Nut Bread

Preheat oven: 350 degrees
Preparation time: 10 minutes, plus 55 minutes bake time
Yield: 1 loaf

1¾ cups sifted flour
¼ teaspoon double acting baking powder
1 teaspoon baking soda
1 teaspoon salt
½ teaspoon ground cinnamon
1⅓ cups sugar
⅓ cup shortening
2 eggs
1 teaspoon vanilla
1 cup mashed avocado
⅓ cup water
½ cup chopped pecans

Sift together flour, baking powder, baking soda, salt and cinnamon. Set aside. Beat together sugar, shortening, eggs and vanilla until light and fluffy. Stir in avocado. Combine flour mixture, sugar mixture and water alternately. Do not overbeat between additions. Fold in nuts. Pour into a greased loaf pan and bake 1 hour.

Cinnamon is dried, ground bark of the cinnamomum cassia tree, which is grown in Vietnam. This rich brown spice has a pungent, bitter flavor. Cinnamon is traditionally used for baking and desserts. For a delightful variety, try using a small amount of cinnamon on meat and seafood.

Avocado Chiffon Pie

Preparation time: 15 minutes, 1 hour 20 minutes chill time
Yield: 1 pie

1 envelope unflavored gelatin
½ cup sugar
2 eggs, separated
1½ cups milk
1 avocado, mashed
⅛ cup lemon juice
1 9 inch baked pie shell
 mint sprigs for garnish

Pour gelatin and sugar into a small sauce pan. Beat egg yolks with milk. Stir into gelatin mixture. Let stand for 2 minutes. Heat gently until sugar and gelatin dissolve. Blend in avocado and lemon juice. Chill for 20 minutes or until mixture mounds slightly on a spoon. Beat egg whites until stiff. Slowly add remaining sugar. Fold into gelatin mixture. Pour into pie shell. Chill until firm (about 1 hour). Garnish with mint sprigs.

Avocado Home Orchard Guide

Avocado trees may grow tall and upright or short and sprawling. These evergreen trees create a dense, shade casting canopy of deep green.

There are three strains of avocados: West Indian, Guatemalan and Mexican. The West Indian strain is frost tender and is not widely grown in the United States. Guatemalan and Mexican strains will grow in the mildest areas of this country.

Hundreds of varieties have been developed from the Mexican and Guatemalan strains. Mexican varieties have hardy rootstocks and can be grown in cooler, coastal areas. Guatemalan varieties are a little more frost tender and should be grown in the warmer, inland areas.

Fruit from avocado trees varies, from large and round, weighing more than two pounds, to small pear shaped fruit weighing a few ounces. Avocados have a smooth buttery texture with a nut-like flavor. They are a highly nutritious fruit.

Climate and Soil Requirements

Avocado trees need subtropical climates. Parts of California, Florida, Hawaii and Texas provide suitable climates for growing avocado trees. Average temperatures above 60 degrees during bloom are necessary for fruit to set. Temperatures that drop below freezing for any period of time will destroy the crop and damage the trees.

Avocados trees grow well in a wide range of soil types, but a coarse-textured soil at least 3 feet deep is best. Select an area that has both good surface drainage and internal drainage. Do not plant trees in clay or hardpan subsoils unless adequate drainage is provided. These soils accumulate subsurface water which restricts root development and tends to cause root rot.

The preferred time for tree planting is mid-March thru May. Trees planted in early spring will be stronger for the coming winter and will bear fruit sooner.

Seedlings

Seedlings may grow into beautiful houseplants but planting seedlings to bear fruit is risky. There is a chance the seedling will not have fruit. If a seedling grown tree bears fruit at all, its fruit is usually different in size and quality from the mother plant. To obtain best results, graft a selected variety scion (a short branch with a few buds) onto the seedling rootstock. This process takes patience and experience. If you have time and space to experiment, you may get lucky. Otherwise, you may enjoy a large, leafy houseplant or outdoor tree.

#1. Carefully wash and dry the avocado seed. With three toothpicks (round ones work best) suspend the seed, broad side down, over a jar or glass. Fill the jar with water until it covers the bottom of the seed, about ½ inch.

#2. Place the seed in a warm location out of direct sunlight. Change the water every few days. Clean water will insure a happy and healthy plant. Within 2 to 6 weeks, the seed will crack and tiny roots and stem will form. If the seed has not cracked after 2 months, discard it and try another seed.

#3. When the stem reaches a height of about 6 inches, cut it back 3 inches with a sharp, clean knife or razor blade. This may seem painful, but the tree will sprout new leaves. This will help the plant grow bushy instead of spindly. Remember to change the water every few days.

#4. After a few months, the avocado plant will need a new, more permanent container. Half fill a 10 inch clay pot with potting soil. Carefully remove the toothpicks from the sides of the seed. Hold the plant in one hand and lower it into the pot. Gently fill in the sides with soil, leaving the top half of the seed exposed. Gently tamp the soil down, be careful not to damage the roots. Set the pot in a draining dish. Pour the water from the jar over the soil. Add more water if necessary to thoroughly wet the soil. Let it stand for 10 to 15 minutes, then pour off any excess water. Never leave the plant sitting in water for much longer than that. Put the plant and its new home in a bright location without direct sunlight. Let the soil dry completely between waterings. After the seedling has developed a strong root system, it may be moved outdoors. Start by taking it outdoors for 2 hours each day for 1 week. Gradually leave it out longer over several weeks until it has adjusted to the new climate. Remember, it may or may not produce avocados.

Predictable quality and quantity of fruit can be obtained from a nursery grafted tree. Selecting a variety that does well in the area will greatly increase the chances of having a healthy, fruit bearing tree. Select a tree that has healed well where it was grafted. Do not select a tree that is weak or has irregular growth on it or is root bound.

When selecting grafted trees, consider fruit maturity. Avocados mature in different seasons. Select several so that fruit will be available year round.

Most varieties will grow 30 feet tall and spread even wider. If garden space is limited, try a dwarfing rootstock. Annually prune and top the tree. This may reduce the crop but will provide fruit in a limited space.

Avocado trees are only partially self pollinating. Avocado varieties can be divided into two types, depending on how and when the flowers open and close. Listed below are a few popular varieties and their characteristics. A local nursery or county extention agent will help you choose the best variety for your area. Selecting trees from both flower types is recommended.

A chart has been prepared using a few common varieties. Compare local varieties to determine suitability.

Variety	Maturity Season	Tree Size	Flower Type	Skin Texture and Color	Fruit Size	
Hass	April to November	Medium & Spreading	A	thick pebbly skin deep purple/black	S-M	
Fuerte	November to June	Large & Spreading	B	medium thin skin - green	S-M	
Bacon	December to March	Tall & Erect	B	thin skin - dark green	M	
Zutano	October to February	Tall & Erect	B	thin shiney skin - light green	M	
Pinkerton	December to March	Medium & Spreading	A	thick pebbly skin - green	M-L	
Reed	July to September	Medium & Erect	A	thick leathery skin - green	L	

S = 3 to 6 oz.   M = 7 to 10 oz.   L = 11 oz. to 2 lbs.

Planting

Start by digging a hole that is the same depth as the soil inside the tree container and 6 to 8 inches wider than the container. If dug too deeply, back filling with the same soil should be well tamped so the tree will not settle and sink.

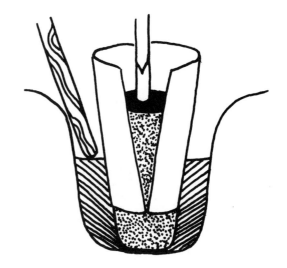

Using a sharp knife or can opener, cut away the bottom of the container and slice the side so the container may be removed after lowering it into the hole.

Place hands firmly on the container, never the tree trunk. Lower it into the hole and remove the container.

Carefully fill in the sides with soil, tamping it as you go. Be careful not to damage the root system. Thoroughly water the newly planted tree, then water again the following day.

Protect the newly planted tree from the sun and wind by wrapping the trunk in a cylinder made of cardboard, newspaper, an empty milk carton or burlap. Tie or staple the cylinder around the bottom of the tree. Never use tar paper or plastic, it will be too hot. Be sure the wrap covers about 10 inches above the graft, leaving plenty of room for the tree to grow. It should not touch the foliage. In windy areas, stake the tree to keep it from breaking, using a 2 inch by 2 inch by 5 foot stake. Tie it with plastic or soft twine. Wire or paper wrapped wire will damage the tree as it grows.

Water the new tree frequently, its root system is limited to the root ball and it will only absorb moisture that comes in direct contact with the root ball. Eventually 75% of an avocado trees' root system develops in the first 2 feet of soil. It is not necessary to water deeper. A young tree will need 7 to 10 gallons of water a week the first summer. Avocados need ample water but do not take well to continuously wet soil either. Hot or windy days will dry the tree out quicker, additional watering may be necessary. Let the soil dry out between waterings but not for any extended period of time.

Irrigation methods

There are several irrigation methods suitable for avocado trees.

Basin: Form a basin around the tree using additional soil (digging around the tree damages surface roots). Make it large enough to hold 5 to 10 gallons of water. Fill the basin with water and let it absorb. During the rainy months to allow excess water to run out, open one side of the basin. The basin method of irrigation is good for the trees first 2 to 3 years, afterward, it will be necessary to convert to another method of irrigation.

Drip: Run a drip line 2 inches from the tree trunk. Place one emitter at each tree during the first year. For the second season, pull the emitter line to 18'' from the tree trunk and place another emitter an equal distance from the tree. In the fourth and fifth season, add 2 more emitters, to total 4 per tree at three foot intervals along the hose. As the tree grows, add more emitters to total 8 to 10. The tree will require 20 to 30 gallons of water per day.

Sprinkler: Use one quarter or one third circle sprinklers placed close to each tree for the first 2 years. Use a one half circle sprinkler and place it several feet away from the trunk to cover a greater portion of the root zone during the third and fourth year. When the tree matures, use full coverage sprinklers.

Hose: Place a hose at the base of the tree with a light even water flow. Move the hose frequently to water all of the surface roots.

Regardless of the irrigation method you use, make sure that your trees are getting enough water. Use a soil probe, an auger or shovel to check the soil for moisture content. Wet soil sticks together, dry soil crumbles. Never water wet soil. Water more often in dry, windy weather.

Mulching and Fertilizing

Weeds around a tree compete for moisture and nutrients. Keep weeds to a minimum and help prevent the evaporation of moisture by mulching, at least 2 inches thick, around the base of the tree. Mulch with fallen leaves, straw or wood shavings. Remember, when hoeing under a tree, be very careful not to damage the surface roots. Herbacides can be used around the tree to eliminate weeds. Check with a nursery for different products on the market. A properly cared for tree should show good growth during the first year or two. A tree that does not appear to be growing well may need more fertilizers. Fertilize lightly and frequently. A local nursery will be able to provide a good "citrus and avocado food" fertilizer or an all purpose fertilizer. Follow the instructions carefully. Try fertilizing the first time you water each month, if it instructs monthly usage. This will help eliminate some of the confusion.

Insecticides

Healthy growing trees seldom suffer from pests. Do not apply insecticides to a tree unnecessarily as it may upset the natural balance between pests and parasites.

Mites, loopers, leafrollers, scale, thrips and fruit flies are the most common of avocado tree pests. Often, pests may be controlled biologically by introducing a parasite specific for that pest. Contact a registered pest control advisor or Extension Advisor for programs in your area.

Pruning

Avocado trees' natural growth habits are irregular and they are ultimately best left unpruned or lightly pruned. Young trees will produce fruit sooner if they are not pruned. If pruning is necessary, it is best for shaping and developing to prune while a tree is still young. A tall tree may be made bushier by pinching or breaking out the growth buds with your thumb and fore-finger. This should be done in the first few years. Be consistent or the buds will grow right back.

It may be necessary to prune a mature tree to keep limbs out of wires or to lighten extremely heavy limbs. Before pruning, be sure that the leaf canopy is dense enough to prevent the trunk or upper limbs from being exposed and sunburnt (sunburn may be prevented by painting the top side of limbs and trunk with a white water base paint). Prune the lateral branches and cut close to the main trunk. Leave as many leaves and as much green wood as possible.

Fruit Maturity

There are many signs an avocado may give to show its maturity. Dark skin varieties turn darker, green skinned fruit sometimes becomes dull and the stems on some will yellow.

The best determination of fruit maturity is to pick a large fruit and take it indoors to ripen. Mature fruit will ripen evenly and consistently in 2 to 10 days. Immature fruit will shrivel and not ripen evenly. The seed covering of an immature fruit will be white and thick, a mature seed will have a thin brown paper shell.

The tree provides the best storage for avocados. The ripening process is triggered when the fruit is picked. Some varieties will hang on the tree for 6 months while others must be picked within a few weeks.

Harvesting

Harvesting avocados from a tall tree requires the use of a pole picker and a ladder. A pole picker may be purchased with clippers and bag already attached. When using a picker without a bag, try having one person cutting the avocado stems and another catching the avocados in a net. A homemade picker can be made by attaching a 1 lb. aluminum can to a bamboo pole and cutting a v notch on the outside rim of the can. Push the can up under the avocado with the stem resting in the v notch, push sharply to slice the stem. It is best to leave a small stem button on the avocado to prevent bacteria from entering and rotting the exposed end.

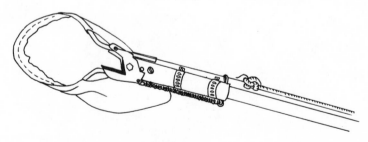

Pole Picker

Home Orchard Problems and Solutions

Problem: Flower Drop

Probable Cause: Frost, too cool and windy or fluctuating temperatures. Avocado trees will shed flowers, but excessive flower drop is not normal. Avocado trees bloom very heavily but only a small percent ever set fruit.

Solution: Normal weather conditions and good care should put the tree back on track for the next season.

Problem: Excessive leaf drop while flowering

Probable Cause: It is common for leaves to drop while flowering. A tree may be without leaves for a brief time, then sprout new growth and be green again within a few weeks.

Problem: Flowers but little or no fruit set.

Probable Cause: Lack of pollination. Individual avocado flowers are not self-pollinating. Avocado varieties are of 2 types of flowers, Type A and Type B. It is necessary to have at least one of each type to insure adequate pollination. Weather and the presence of pollinating insects may also effect pollination.

Solution: Try grafting a bearing scion (short branch with buds) of the opposite flower type onto the tree or plant a tree of the opposite flower type in the same area. Bees and wasps help pollination. Consider getting a beehive.

Problem: Small finger shaped fruits.

Probable Causes: Fluctuating temperatures or drying winds can cause what are called "cukes" or "cocktail" avocados to form. They are fruit that develop after the seed dies or fails to form.

Solution: Provide adequate water and good maintainance for the tree. Favorable weather should return the fruit to normal. Meanwhile, ripen and enjoy the seedless fruit. These tiny avocados sell for a premium at the supermarket.

Problem: corky brown spots on fruit and branches

Probable Causes: These spots are caused by sunburn, limb rub or over maturity of some varieties. These spots lower the market value of the fruit but may not affect the interior quality.

Solution: Pick the fruit as it matures, affected fruit doesn't keep well.

Problem: Dying, dropping leaves with burnt brown tips.

Probable Causes: Inadequate watering, dry winds or too much salt in the soil.

Solution: Water as soon as the soil is dry. Check the soil with a soil auger at 18-24 inches deep weekly. Water excessively heavily once every few months to leach excess salt from the soil. Consider adding more drip emitters, or changing to a larger sprinkle, or irrigating more frequently.

Problem: Yellow leaves

Probable Causes: New leaves that turn yellow and mature leaves that are overall bright yellow and full sized may indicate chlorosis, an iron deficiency. This deficiency is caused by excess lime in the soil (too much calcium) or excess moisture, or both.

Solution: Keep trees on a regular watering schedule. Water to a depth of 2 feet as soon as the soil is dry. (Check the drip line with a soil auger at 18-24 inches deep, weekly). Apply chelated iron around the root system. Follow instructions given on package.

Problem: Lack of vegetation, small pale leaves

Probable Causes: Chronic water shortage or a nitrogen deficiency.

Solution: Keep trees on a regular watering schedule. Water to a depth of 2 feet as soon as the soil is dry. (Check the drip line with a soil auger at 18-24 inches deep weekly). Nitrogen is the major nutrient avocados need. Fertilize lightly. Use "citrus and avocado food" or an all purpose fertilizer. Follow the package instructions carefully, as avocado root systems are easily damaged by fertilizers.

Problem: Mottled leaves with light green to pale yellow areas between the veins and burns on outer edges, new leaves are smaller

Probable Causes: Zinc deficiency.

Solution: The problem may be controlled by applying zinc spray to the foliage or in some soils (those with acid reactions) by applying zinc sulfate to the soil. Both methods should be done carefully following package instructions.

Problem: Pale, droopy leaves, top branches dying back, roots decaying and turning black, overall tree deteriorating

Probable Causes: Cinnamon Fungas (Phytophthora cinnamomi), also known as root rot.

Solution: It is the worst problem avocado tree growers face. There is no complete remedy for root rot, because it stays in the soil and is not easily cured. Reduce the chance of infecting unaffected areas by careful watering. Never water wet soil and divert run-off water so as not to increase spread. When planting new trees, purchase "root rot resistant" rootstock.

Retail bookstores and wholesalers may order copies of *The Avocado Lover's Cookbook* in quantity from *Celestial Arts,* P.O. Box 7327, Berkeley, CA 94707. Or call (415) 524-1801 to discuss our terms (which are most agreeable).

Celestial Arts publishes fine cookbooks and self-help books in the areas of spiritual growth, inspiration, popular psychology, health and wellness, children's, and posters/graphics. Please write for our free catalog.

Celestial Arts is a part of the total publishing program of *Ten Speed Press. Ten Speed's* list includes the bestselling WHAT COLOR IS YOUR PARACHUTE? and LADIES' OWN EROTICA, as well as a fine list of cookbooks including the vegetarian classic THE MOOSE-WOOD COOKBOOK. *Ten Speed's* catalog is available by writing us at P.O. Box 7123, Berkeley, CA 94707 or call (415) 845-8414.

MAY WE INTRODUCE YOU? . . .

to *The Artichoke Cookbook,* by Patricia Rain.
   More than 100 recipes plus folklore and history of this unique and beloved vegetable. 174 pages, with beautiful illustrations and index. Paperbound $8.95. Available from *Celestial Arts.*

to *The Garlic Lovers' Cookbook.*
   More than 200 recipes from the Gilroy Garlic Festival, including recipes from Italy, France, China, Mexico, and the United States. 176 pages, with drawings and index. Paperbound $6.95, spiral-bound $9.95. Available from *Celestial Arts.*

to *The Garlic Lovers' Cookbook, Volume II.*
   More new, original recipes from the Gilroy Garlic Festival. 192 pages, with line drawings. Paperbound $7.95, spiral-bound $10.95. Available from *Celestial Arts.*

INDIVIDUAL ORDERS:

Send a note indicating the number of copies you'd like, the address you'd like them sent to, and a check for the appropriate amount to *Blue Ribbon Publishers,* P.O. Box 6738-200, Santa Barbara, CA 93160. Make your check payable to *Blue Ribbon Publishers,* and if you are a California resident, please add 60¢ tax for each copy ordered. Everyone should add $1.00 shipping charges for the first copy and 50¢ each additional book. Each copy is $9.95 apiece, plus the shipping and tax (if applicable) as shown above.

Order Form

Blue Ribbon Publishers
P.O. Box 6738-200
Santa Barbara, CA 93160

Please send me_____copy(ies) of *The Avocado Lover's Cookbook* by Joyce Carlisle.

    × $9.95 Price per Book

$_____Total for Books

_____Shipping Charges (@$1.00 shipping first book
50¢ each additional book)

_____California residents please add 6% sales tax

$_____Total Amount Enclosed

I understand that I may return the book(s) for a full refund if not satisfied.

Name:_____

Street Address:_____

City:_____State:_____Zip:_____